To Paul —
With warmest !
best wishes

3/10/88

A HOUSE

Pat Swindall

A congressman examines the divisive
issues that face America today.

DIVIDED

OLIVER
NELSON

A Division of Thomas Nelson Publishers
Nashville

Published in Nashville, Tennessee, by Oliver-Nelson
Books, a division of Thomas Nelson, Inc., Publishers, and
distributed in Canada by Lawson Falle, Ltd.,
Cambridge, Ontario.

Scripture quotations are from The King James Version
of the Holy Bible.

Printed in the United States.

Library of Congress Cataloging-in-Publication Data

Swindall, Pat, 1950–
    A house divided : a congressman examines the divisive
issues that face America today / Pat Swindall.
        p.   cm.
    Bibliography: p.
    ISBN 0-8407-9079-1 : $12.95
    1. United States—Constitutional history.   2. Federal
government—United States.   3. United States—Politics
and government—1981–   . I. Title.
JK261.S94   1988
973.927—dc19   87–27895
                                                              CIP

1 2 3 4 5 6 — 92 91 90 89 88 87

Acknowledgments

For their encouragement and advice in assembling much of the material upon which this book is based, I would like to express my sincere appreciation to Tim Crater, Carol Pittman, Dr. Vance Grant, Jan Fujiwara, Pete McLain, Thomas Jacobson, Blair Cunningham, Steve Long, and Allen Taylor.

I would also like to thank Sam Moore, Victor Oliver, and Lila Empson for their encouragement, patience, helpfulness, and cooperation. To our Founders and the numerous writers whom I quote, I owe much. Finally, to my constituents who have honored me by allowing me to represent them in Congress, I express my heartfelt appreciation.

To my wife, Kim, and our greatest blessings, our children

Contents

Figures

Introduction:

TAMPERING WITH THE "REAL THING"

As America celebrates the bicentennial of its Constitution, I'm reminded of another centennial celebration not long ago, that of Coca Cola. Because I grew up in Atlanta, the international headquarters of Coca Cola, and have been an avid and loyal Coke drinker for as long as I can remember, I closely followed the events connected with Coke's grand celebration. Though this event was a smashing success, it came dangerously close to being a total disaster, because in 1985, the year before its centennial, the Coca Cola Company made a monumental and earth-shaking decision. It decided to change its famous, original formula.

After years of marketing research, the management of Coke decided that, as good as the original formula was, it should be changed. In short, it had become convinced that by changing the formula, it could improve its marketing share in its second 100 years. With great fanfare, Coca Cola announced its decision to shelve the original Coca Cola formula and introduce a new one.

I can still vividly recall where I was when I learned of the change. I was in the Republican cloakroom, located in the Capitol adjacent to the House Chamber, when one of my colleagues asked me what I thought of Coke's decision to change formulas. At first, I thought he was kidding. As he persisted, I realized he wasn't. I immediately called a friend who worked with Coke and asked him if the rumor was true. My heart sank as he confirmed the story. After hanging up the phone, I remember thinking to myself, *This new formula had better be good*.

PUBLIC REACTION

In the weeks that followed, the public reacted with outrage. Many complained that the new formula tasted too much like Pepsi. Others thought it was just a clever marketing strategy to get folks to clamor for the return of the old formula. As the public outrage continued, the executives at Coke called a press conference to dispel rumors that the old formula would return. The gist of the press conference was that management had made its decision and the corporate officers intended to stick by it.

As the summer progressed, the marketing data confirmed my initial hunch—Coke had made a huge mistake. The public literally was not buying Coca Cola's decision.

As the plans for the centennial celebration began to finalize, the management at Coke grew increasingly worried about the results of their decision. What were they to do? As the world focused its attention on Atlanta and the centennial celebration, the talk centered more on the disaster of new Coke than on the festivities designed to recognize the success of the soft drink industry's giant.

It was under these circumstances that the management at Coke met to try to salvage not just the centennial celebration, but also the future of Coca Cola itself. Fortunately for the thousands who owned stock in Coca Cola and the millions who saw Coca Cola more as a legend than as a soft drink, management made the right decision. Rather than continuing down the road to probable failure, they reversed their course and made a conscious and courageous decision to re-embrace the philosophy and original formula that had been responsible for their past, unparalleled growth and success. Coca Cola's management decided to return to "the real thing."

Immediately before the centennial celebration began, management implemented its decision by reintroducing the original formula as "Coke Classic." With that decision made, the centennial celebration was a glowing success and, more importantly for the company, Coke rapidly reclaimed its position of dominance in the soft drink industry.

THE NATIONAL PARALLEL

The parallels between Coke's centennial and the bicentennial of our Constitution are striking. As we celebrate our two-hundredth birthday as a constitutional republic, we have an unprecedented opportunity to reexamine the philosophy and formula responsible for our unparalleled success as a nation. Like the management of Coca Cola, we know that while we can't fully understand all the reasons for the success of our original philosophy, as expressed in the Declaration of Independence and in our original formula, the Constitution, we can certainly recognize that it has worked, and worked well.

But like Coca Cola, we as a people have altered our original, winning formula. As a lawyer, a businessman, and as a United States congressman, I have come to believe that one of the most serious problems we face today is that we have gradually drifted away from our original, constitutional framework. This drift has been subtle as well as gradual, and for that reason the more difficult to detect.

Whether consciously or unconsciously, we've tampered with "the real thing." This is why, for instance, Attorney General Edwin Meese and a host of others have been stirring up the debate about the "original intent" of the Founders, their meanings when they first penned the Constitution. Increasingly, the courts and other state institutions have played fast and loose with our founding principles and the "formula" that implements them, saying it is a "dynamic" document. That's frequently just another way of saying it is their right to alter the Constitution as they see fit.

It was the chief architect of the Constitution himself, James Madison, who insisted to the contrary that "it was the duty of all to support the Constitution in its true meaning as understood by the Nation at the time of its ratification."[1] He, for one, did not view the document as being so fluid that its meaning could be as easily distorted as we are seeing done today. Madison was not saying the Constitution isn't a dynamic document. Rather, he was saying it *is* dynamic, but that there's a well-devised, carefully constructed mechanism for the expression of its dynamism.

The mechanism Madison and the other original writers had in mind is the amendment process that's part of the constitutional framework. It's a process whereby the people themselves, in a deliberative and democratic fashion, may continue to be their own rulers. The courts were not given this right, nor was the Congress. Their actions, in tampering with our original, winning formula by reinterpreting it, were not only never intended by the Founders, but were wholly unforeseen by them.

In this regard, it is therefore not surprising that a Supreme Court justice recently came right out and said that he didn't think the Constitution was such a great document, that it was defective from the start.

RESTORING THE FOUNDERS' FORMULA

Count me among those who want to issue a clear call for a return to "the real thing" in constitutional government, to the original intent of the Founders, and to their way of amending the rules of our national life, a way that respects the people's right to rule themselves and that protects them from the caprice of government officials, including the courts.

I believe the Founders captured some timeless truths in our founding documents, truths such as human freedom and representative government, which should never be changed or tampered with. But I believe they also recognized that there would be a need to change certain things, to adapt these timeless truths to the times, or else they would not have built in the amendment process. I am seriously concerned, however, that we have strayed from those timeless truths, and that our fundamental law is being changed in an illicit manner.

It is my hope that we can take this historic opportunity to learn from our mistakes and admit that we have acted unwisely in abandoning a winning formula. Like Coke, we've tried to fix something that wasn't broken.

Nineteen eighty-eight will mark the midpoint of our bicentennial celebration. It can, however, be much more. It can be a turning point in our national history, a unique opportunity to relearn (the polls show a serious public ignorance of our own Constitution) and reembrace the philosophy and formula that have made the United States of America the greatest success story in the history of the world. The Founders gave us a winning formula, and I hope we will have the good sense to return to it.

In the succeeding pages of this book, I will show how we've departed from our original heritage and the consequences of that departure in key areas of our national life. More importantly, I will show how we can all benefit from recapturing our original philosophy and returning to "the real thing" in constitutional government.

1

Diagnosing the Real Problem

*T*he key to solving any problem is knowing what the real problem is. In problem solving there is always the potential of focusing on the various symptoms rather than the problem itself. When that happens, the underlying situation can, and usually does, become significantly worse.

A PERSONAL DIAGNOSIS

My first understanding of dealing symptomatically with a problem occurred during the summer of 1965, when I was fifteen years old. During my summer recess, I worked at my father's used furniture store in downtown Atlanta, as I had always done on Saturdays and during summer recesses and other school holidays. As usual, my duties consisted of delivering furniture that had been sold at our store or picking up used furniture that had been purchased from various private homes and hotels or motels around town.

Unlike previous summer recesses, however, during the summer of 1965 I found myself physically worn out all the time. At first I thought it was due to the extremely high temperatures that characterized the summer of '65, or to the fact that during that summer the work had been more strenuous than usual because we had purchased all the furniture in a downtown hotel that was scheduled for demolition. As the summer went on, I found that in addition to being weak, my stomach ached and I was regularly getting light-headed. Frequently, when I would climb out of the pickup truck after riding from one delivery stop to the next, I would nearly faint.

Because my condition was becoming increasingly obvious to those around me, especially the delivery-man with whom I worked and my older brother, they began to ask me what was wrong. When I told them I was tired and my stomach hurt, numerous diagnoses and suggestions were made. The deliveryman was convinced that I was staying up too late at night, but I knew I was going to bed at the same time that I had during previous summers. My brother suggested I had an upset stomach because of the hot dogs and delica-tessen sandwiches I ate during the day. Again, this made no sense, because I had always eaten hot dogs and delicatessen sandwiches when I worked at my father's store.

As the summer continued and I became weaker and my light-headedness and stomach aches worsened, I began to go to bed very early at night, even before dark. I also began to skip meals and drink soft drinks in hopes of settling my stomach. None of these reme-dies seemed to help.

Then early one morning when I was on my way to the bathroom to get some water (I had been unusually thirsty all summer), I passed out on the floor in the hall of my family's home. Fortunately, the glass I was carrying broke and the noise caused my parents to come downstairs to investigate. When they found me, I was sprawled on the floor, out like a light. Though I had only partially regained consciousness, I can still remember hearing my parents and brothers and sister clamoring around me. "What's wrong?" "You know he's been acting funny all summer." And finally, "Call an ambulance, we've got to get him to a doctor."

The next thing I remember was a doctor's holding smelling salts under my nose and asking me to describe what had happened. After I told him how I had been feeling that summer and what I had been doing to treat myself, he immediately concluded that I was anemic. That is to say, I had a bleeding ulcer and had lost so much blood that I had passed out. Had I not gotten to the doctor when I did I could have died, not from the ulcer but from the loss of blood.

After admitting me to the hospital, my doctor explained that my ulcer, which was nothing more than a hole in the lining of my stomach, had caused bleeding because it was located on a blood vessel in my stomach. Because I hadn't known what was wrong with me, the ulcer had grown in size and had finally hemorrhaged.

I had always heard that ulcers were caused by eating spicy foods and worrying too much. As we talked, I learned that ulcers are really caused by too much acid being produced by the vagus nerve. The purpose of the nerve is to release the proper amount of acid after a person eats to help the body digest the food that has been consumed. If the nerve causes too much acid to be released, the acid, after all the food is digested, will begin to digest the stomach lining. Spicy foods and worry can cause the vagus nerve to release even more acid, but the real problem is in the vagus nerve itself.

After the doctor explained what was wrong with me, I realized that many of the things I had done during the summer in hopes of helping my condition had actually worsened it. For example, drinking carbonated soft drinks didn't settle my stomach as I had hoped, but rather increased the acidity level in my empty stomach. Similarly, by my skipping meals, the acid digested my stomach lining rather than the food that would have otherwise been present. Treating my symptoms without understanding the real problem had made it worse rather than better.

The doctor explained that a number of things could be done to properly treat the ulcer symptomatically, including regulation of my diet and eating schedule. By keeping milk in my stomach or something else that would keep the stomach lined, the problem might be controlled. There were, however, some side effects and potential problems with such a treatment program.

First, too much milk could cause calcium deposits that could in turn cause kidney stones or bone problems. Second, if another ulcer did develop, it could occur on a larger blood vessel and result in an uncontrollable hemorrhage.

The only way to solve the real problem was a surgical procedure in which the vagus nerve would be severed and the acid discharge drastically decreased. In a nutshell, my doctor was saying that the acid in my stomach, so long as it was controlled properly, was not only healthy but essential to the digestive process. If, however, the acid could not be controlled by proper symptomatic treatment, a remedial operation would be required.

After eight consecutive years of symptomatic treatment and five separate hemorrhaging episodes, my doctor performed the operation he had originally described, known as a vagotomy. Since the operation I have never experienced another ulcer.

A NATIONAL DIAGNOSIS

Just as it was necessary for me to have my medical problem properly diagnosed and treated, so, too, must we as a nation properly diagnose our real problem. Should we fail to do so, we will almost certainly continue to treat only the symptoms. The problem is that a symptomatic treatment plan not only fails to cure the underlying problem, but it also leaves open the possibility of an outright hemorrhage that could prove fatal.

The Real Problem

An examination of our recent history indicates that we have, in fact, failed to properly diagnose our real problem. For too long we have focused primarily on the symptoms. Our national debt, our continuing annual deficits, growing welfare dependency, the mediocrity of public education, and a diminishing First Amendment in America are all just symptoms of the real problem.

The real problem is the uncontrolled growth of our federal government. Just as the right amount of stomach acid is healthy and essential to a person's body, so, too, is the right amount of federal government healthy for our national life. Conversely, too much acid or too much federal government is not only unhealthy, but even potentially fatal.

The Right Amount of Government

Our Founders understood the necessity of striking a balance between too little and too much federal government. When they gathered in Philadelphia in 1787, they met to address the national crisis that had resulted from the too-little federal government existing under the Articles of Confederation. In the preamble to the Constitution, which resulted from that historic convention, the Founders stated their first purpose in writing a new Constitution: "to form a more perfect union." Their desire then was to create a new order in which the federal government had just the right amount of power and authority, not too little and not too much.

The Constitution is a well-drafted, well-considered document designed to achieve and maintain just the right balance. Contained in the document are numerous checks and balances to prevent any unauthorized growth or shrinkage in the size or scope of the federal government. A key concept incorporated in the document was that of "federalism." The idea is that various, otherwise-independent political units (in the case of our country, these political units are the states) surrender by contract their individual sovereignty to a central government to accomplish certain stated objectives. All the powers not specifically surrendered under the terms of the contract are retained by the various political units.

Under such an arrangement, if properly drawn and adhered to, the right balance is struck between the federal government on the one hand and the states and the people on the other. A failure to adhere to the agreement has severe and sometimes castastrophic consequences. In the case of our own nation, these consequences are leading to national frustration and an unhealthy and unnecessary division between our leaders and our populace. In the following chapters, a number of the more glaring consequences, or symptoms, if you will, of our nation's having strayed from the terms of our original agreement will be examined. My hope is that we, the people of the United States, will, after examining the symptoms, arrive at the correct diagnosis. Then, more importantly, we must take the right cure.

2

Symptom: A Failure to Establish Justice

Our nation today is more deeply divided than it has been at any time since the troublesome days of Abraham Lincoln's presidency. The issues that divide us may appear, at least superficially, to be quite different from the ones that divided us in 1860. There might seem to be little, if any, connection between the issue of slavery and issues like prayer in school, abortion, capital punishment, a growing welfare state, an overwhelming national debt, and constantly declining educational achievement scores.

These issues are related, however, in a very direct and significant manner. All are symptoms of an extremely important, underlying conflict. Abraham Lincoln recognized this conflict when on June 16, 1858, he accepted his party's nomination as its candidate for the U.S. Senate from the state of Illinois. In addressing the closing session of the Republican state convention that nominated him, Lincoln borrowed a phrase from Scripture to state the theme of his unsuccessful campaign. Two years later, he repeated this same theme in his successful campaign for president of the United States. The phrase he borrowed was from Christ's message to the Pharisees nearly two thousand years earlier: "A house divided against itself cannot stand" (see Matthew 12:25). In that same speech, Lincoln predicted that "this government cannot endure permanently half slave and half free. I do not expect the Union to be dissolved—I do not expect the house to fall—but I do expect it will cease to be divided. It will become all one thing, or all the other."[1]

As we now know, both of Lincoln's predictions came true. Our nation did survive, though it was tested to the point of near destruction. Equally significant was that one view prevailed to the exclusion of the other, the view that slavery was wrong and could no longer be tolerated by a government founded on the constitutional principle that no citizen could be deprived of his or her right to freedom without due process of law.

On the surface, Lincoln was addressing the issue of slavery. Beneath the surface, he was addressing a much more fundamental conflict. It is the same conflict that has raged since time eternal. It is a conflict between two mutually exclusive and irreconcilable world views.

The first world view is the one embraced by our Founding Fathers when they wrote the Declaration of Independence and the Constitution. It recognizes the existence and relevance of the laws our Founders called "the laws of Nature and Nature's God." It is a world view in which God, not man, is the ultimate and supreme authority.

The other world view is the converse of the Founders'. It's one embraced by many of those who, in the name of interpretation and loose construction of the Declaration of Independence and Constitution, are now subtly rewriting these documents and the underlying principles upon which they are based. It's a world view in which there are no absolutes or standards because man is the ultimate and supreme authority.

These two world views cannot coexist. One will eventually survive to the exclusion of the other, and the one that survives will determine the type of nation in which our children and our children's children will live. To understand these world views and the natural consequences of each is the key not only to understanding many of the divisive issues currently being debated in America today, but also to resolving them.

As we celebrate the bicentennial of our nation's Constitution, it is essential that we recognize that we have ever so gradually, without any significant deliberation, drifted away from the world view that our Founding Fathers decided, after *great* deliberation, to incorporate in the two documents that make up our foundation. It is on this foundation that we have built our nation.

It is not, however, too late to reestablish this foundation by returning to the philosophy that has served us so well in the past. Should we decide to abandon that philosophy and replace it with another, we ought to at least make such a change with great deliberation and public debate. Such a debate must necessarily focus on the real issue, the choice between the conflicting world views to which Lincoln referred over 100 years ago.

There is no more appropriate time than the present to begin that debate. The logical place to begin is with an examination of our Constitution and the Declaration of Independence. In those two documents the Founders resolved this conflict in world views, and how they went about it can serve as an example for us in deciding the issues that divide us today.

MIXING RELIGION
AND POLITICS

In resolving this conflict, the Founders addressed an issue that still divides us today, the issue of mixing politics and religion. Both the Declaration of Independence and the Constitution reflect a necessary understanding of the fact that it's only a half-truth to say it's improper to mix politics and religion. It is true only in the sense that *how* one goes about worshiping (or, for that matter, not worshiping) a supreme being has no place in politics or civil government. For example, whether John Kennedy, a devout Roman Catholic, made a practice of saying the rosary or going to a priest to make a confession was an irrelevant and inappropriate political issue. To even discuss such an issue in the context of a political race is dangerous and unnecessarily divisive.

The Founders understood that it is also improper and ill-advised to mix religion and politics in the sense of using civil government to force certain principles or styles of worship on others. There were those in 1787, just as there are now, who wanted our nation to be a theocracy, where various blue laws and other requirements concerning practices of worship and other aspects of humanity's relationship with God are forced upon the populace by the civil government. In 1787 several states had already established theocratic governments at the state level. Our Founders wisely resisted the temptation to establish a national theocratic government, because they knew the end result would be a loss of religious freedom.

They knew that all freedoms, including our freedom of religion, can be achieved only when civil government establishes and enforces laws designed to recognize and protect the fundamental rights spelled out in the Declaration of Independence and Constitution. Those rights deal with the relationships between people in civil society. In determining which rights are to be recognized and protected, they knew it was absolutely *necessary* to mix religion and politics. It is in this sense that the assertion that it's improper to mix religion and politics is wholly untrue. Religion, in the sense that it means a system of values and beliefs as opposed to how or even whether one worships God, *must* be discussed in the context of politics and civil government. In fact, in this sense of the word, it is impossible not to mix religion and politics.

Because civil government must reflect someone's

values and beliefs, the only relevant question becomes, "Whose values and beliefs?" Ideally, the purpose of the electoral process is to allow voters to discern the values and beliefs of the candidates who aspire to serve in public office. After making such a discernment, voters inevitably choose those candidates who most reflect their own values and beliefs. In the process, however, voters need not delve into the irrelevant and inappropriate issue of how or whether a candidate worships a supreme being. A meaningful assessment of the values and beliefs of a particular candidate can be made without engaging in such an examination.

The writers of the Declaration of Independence and the Constitution understood this critical distinction between the relevant and the irrelevant, as well as between the proper and the improper. And because they did, they were able to demonstrate by example how to incorporate into the fiber of our civil government the aspect of religion that's relevant to the political process. They also wisely avoided incorporating any irrelevant aspect of religion that is related to how or whether an individual chooses to worship a supreme being.

THE WORLD VIEW OF
THE FOUNDERS

Because our Founders understood that neither civil government nor politics can exist devoid of religious content, the principles they included in the Declaration of Independence make it as much a theological document as a political one.

In fact, a careful examination of the Declaration reveals that the Founders stated their political and religious justification for the revolution they knew was inevitable. Specifically, they stated why they were justified in revolting against the established government of Great Britain. The need to do this was in large part due to the theology of those of the Founders who were Christians. Undoubtedly these men were concerned about the admonition contained in the New Testament book of Romans, chapter 13, verses 1 and 2:

> Let every soul be subject unto the higher powers. For there is no power but of God: The powers that be are ordained of God. Whosoever therefore resisteth the power, resisteth the ordinance of God: and they that resist shall receive to themselves damnation.

Nowhere is their concern more evident than in that portion of the Declaration of Independence where they politically and theologically justified the American Revolution:

> We hold these Truths to be self-evident, that all Men are created equal, that they are endowed by their Creator with certain unalienable Rights, that among these are Life, Liberty and the Pursuit of Happiness—That to secure these Rights, Governments are instituted among Men, deriving their just Powers from the Consent of the Governed—that whenever any Form of the Government becomes destructive of these Ends, it is the Right of the People to alter or to abolish it, and to institute new Government, laying its Foundation on such principles. . . .

Agreement on Principles

In addition to stating their theological and political justification for the American Revolution, the Founders stated in the Declaration of Independence those principles upon which they could all agree. The Declaration and the Constitution have survived the test of time primarily because of the Founders' decision to focus on the principles upon which they could all agree rather than upon the principles over which they differed. The principles upon which they could all agree were important because each of those principles had consequences that profoundly affected the civil government they formed.

First Principle: A Creator

The first principle upon which they could all agree was that there exists a Creator, to whom they refer in the first sentence of the Declaration as "Nature's God." In their words, the existence of the Creator is "self-evident." In making this declaration, the Founders wisely avoided going any further theologically than was absolutely necessary to achieve their purpose. Their choice of words in referring to the Creator reflects this decision.

Second Principle: Providence

In addition to referring to the Creator as "Nature's God," they also made reference in the final portion of the Declaration to the "divine Providence." Their choice of the word *Providence* is significant because (according to *Webster's Ninth New Collegiate Dictionary*) when capitalized, the word *Providence* means a "divine guidance or care" or "God conceived as the power sustaining and guiding human destiny." In other words, by specifying divine Providence, the Founders acknowledged not only the existence of a Creator, but also the Creator's relevance in the affairs of humanity. After agreeing that there is a God, they wisely sought the widest rather than the narrowest possible definition of who God is. In so doing they molded the broadest possible consensus without in the process compromising the one choice that had to be made and made conclusively.

Their Choice of World Views

The choice that had to be made was a choice between two world views, a world view in which God is the ultimate authority or a world view in which man is the ultimate authority. Stated differently, the fundamental issue was from what source their new government would claim its power and scope of responsibility. In fact, the word *authority* means "source." The word *author,* as in the author of a book, comes from the same root word. By deciding that God is the source, or author, of life, the issue was settled. This resolution was important because each of the two world views is mutually exclusive, and because each has inescapable and inevitable consequences.

The natural consequence of a God-centered world view is that the unalienable rights to which the Founders referred are derived from God rather than from the state or its people. Had the Founders chosen to deny either the existence or the relevence of God, the rights to which they referred would not have been "unalienable," because the source of their rights would then have necessarily been man and could be given and taken away by man through the state. The Founders' decision was also significant because it stood in bold and refreshing contrast to the premise of the European governments with which they were all intimately familiar. In the European models of government, the rights of the people were granted to them under the authority of the crown.

For the Founding Fathers to conclude that these rights are granted directly to the people under the authority of the Creator and that civil government, if it is to be legitimate, has the God-given responsibility of protecting those rights, was a radical statement, to say the least. What could be more radical than publicly stating that any failure by civil government to satisfy this fundamental responsibility justifies its being altered or abolished by the people? In delineating the rights that the federal government was obligated to protect, the Founders singled out two specifically, the right to life and the right to liberty. A third right, the right to the pursuit of happiness, was stated more generally and was intented to be all-encompassing.

Contributions of Blackstone and Locke

The Founders' statements concerning the origin of these rights and the responsibility of civil government regarding them reflected the principles set forth in a book that was widely circulated in the colonies at that time. This book, *Commentaries on the Laws of England,* was written by William Blackstone and published between 1765 and 1770. Though the book was popular in Great Britain, it was even more popular in the colonies. In fact, by 1775, more copies had been sold in America than in all of England. In his treatise, Blackstone stated that all human laws are derived from one of two foundations. The first foundation is the law of nature, and the second is the law of revelation. Specifically, Blackstone said:

> The doctrines thus delivered we call the revealed or divine law, and they are to be found only in holy scriptures.
> Upon these two foundations, the law of nature and the law of revelation, depend all human laws; that is to say, no human laws should be suffered to contradict these.[2]

Blackstone's influence on the Declaration of Independence can be further seen in these thoughts expressed in his treatise:

> Man, considered as a creature, must necessarily be subject to the laws of his Creator, for he is entirely a dependent being. . . . And, consequently,

as man depends absolutely upon his Maker for everything, it is necessary that he should in all points conform to his Maker's will.[3]

The natural rights philosophy of Blackstone and the Founders had originally been developed and refined by political philosophers such as the Englishman John Locke. Locke, who died in 1704, had a profound impact on the Founders. This can be seen by examining his statement that "the state of nature has a law of nature to govern it which obliges everyone . . . no one ought to harm another in his life, health, liberty, or possessions."

Self-Evidency of a Creator

The words of the Declaration of Independence regarding "the laws of nature and of nature's God" and the self-evidency of certain truths equally reflect Paul's theological argument in Romans 1, where he states in verses 19–20:

Because that which may be known of God is manifest in them; for God hath showed it unto them. For the invisible things of him from the creation of the world are clearly seen, being understood by the things that are made, even his eternal power and Godhead; so that they are without excuse.

In essence, Paul was arguing that when it comes to knowledge about the existence of a Creator, we are all without excuse because His existence is made manifest by the creation itself. In other words, the creation could not logically exist without the prior existence of a Creator. The self-evidency of a Creator is analogous to the obvious fact that a building such as the Capitol of the United States gives indisputable evidence of the prior existence of an architect; such complex buildings do not come into being by accident. Any logical, rational person must necessarily conclude that any structure the size of our Capitol, with sophisticated electrical, plumbing, air conditioning and heating, communications, and interior design systems could not simply have come together randomly. To ask people to believe such a thing would be to ask them to embrace an utter absurdity.

The same logical process leads us to conclude that given the infinitely greater complexity of our cosmos, there must necessarily exist a Creator who planned and made it. The same logic also leads us to conclude that our nation's Capitol simply could not have always existed. There must have been a first cause. So, too, with our cosmos.

It was the same line of reasoning that led the Founding Fathers to conclude it is self-evident that there exists a Creator and that this same Creator is sovereign over every aspect of creation, including the affairs of humanity and the various governments established by God to bring order to the creation.

THE CONSTITUTION: PRACTICAL APPLICATION OF PRINCIPLES

Just as the success of the American Revolution cannot be fully understood or appreciated without an understanding of the ideals and principles set forth in the Declaration of Independence, neither can the success of our nation be understood without a thorough understanding of the Constitution. Simply stated, the Constitution is merely the implementation of the ideals and principles expressed in the Declaration of Independence. In the preamble of the Constitution, the Founders summarized their purpose in writing the Constitution:

We the people of the United States, in order to form a more perfect union, establish justice, insure domestic tranquility, provide for the common defense, promote the general welfare, and secure the blessings of liberty to ourselves and our posterity, do ordain and establish this Constitution for the United States of America.

According to the preamble, our Constitution is a contract, an agreement between "we the people" and the government "we the people" established for the purpose of protecting the rights our Creator gave us. To allow the newly created federal government to achieve this purpose, certain powers had to be granted by the people and assumed by the federal government. The powers given to the federal government were to be few and limited. According to the Tenth Amendment to the Constitution, "The powers not delegated to the United States by the Constitution, are prohibited by it to the states and are reserved to the states respectively, or to the people."

Stated in more modern language, the purpose of our federal government was to establish and maintain law and order, to foster a framework of freedom and security in which people might live out their lives as they saw best. Rexford Tugwell, a close associate of President Franklin Roosevelt during the era of the New Deal, had this to say about the role of government as the Founders viewed it:

The Constitution was a negative document, meant mostly to protect citizens from their government. . . . Above all, men were to be free to do as they liked, and since the government was likely to intervene and because prosperity was to be found in the free management of their affairs, a constitution was needed to prevent such intervention. . . . The laws would maintain order but would not touch the individual who behaved reasonably.[4]

The Constitution established a government, then, that was to create and sustain an orderly society. But it also sought to protect the individual from that same government, which according to Tugwell was "likely to intervene" in their lives and interfere with the "free management of their affairs" unless restrained by statute. This is actually what is involved in the "establishment of justice."

Webster's Ninth New Collegiate Dictionary defines *justice* as "the maintenance or administration of what is just." The same dictionary then defines the word *just* to be that which is "morally upright or good" or "conforming to a standard of correctness."

By What Standard?

Obviously the federal government could not establish a system of justice without first deciding upon what "standard of correctness" it would be based. That question was, of course, necessarily a religious one, because in selecting a standard they were deciding upon whose system of values and beliefs the questions of right and wrong would be determined.

To make that decision, the Founders drew on one of the principles they had stated in the Declaration of Independence. Specifically, they again embraced a world view in which God, not man, is the ultimate authority. Put another way, they chose as their standard the laws of nature and nature's God. No one explained more clearly that this choice was made than did James Madison, the "Father of our Constitution," who in 1788 stated,

We have staked the whole future of the American civilization, not upon the power of government,

far from it. We have staked the future . . . upon
the capacity of each and all of us to govern ourselves, to control ourselves, to sustain ourselves
according to the Ten Commandments of God.[5]

In deciding which of the Ten Commandments
would be enforced by our federal civil government,
the Founders once again differentiated between the
appropriate, those commandments that deal with one
person's relationship to another (no killing, no stealing, etc.), and the inappropriate (no other gods, no
graven image, etc.). The enforcement of the four commandments that deal with our·relationship to God
were left to the institution of the church. To have done
otherwise would have resulted in the establishment of
a theocracy and destroyed the very important objective of our Founders to allow total freedom of religion.

Our civil and criminal laws are replete with evidence that our Founders decided to base our civil and
criminal laws on the appropriate commandments and
Judeo-Christian principles incorporated in the Bible.
Our bankruptcy laws, for example, allow an individual to be adjudicated bankrupt only once every seven
years, thus recognizing the Old Testament principle
that required debt forgiveness every seven years. Similarly, our laws against murder and the appropriate
punishment for murder reflect the Old Testament
principle that premeditated murder is to be treated
differently from unpremeditated murder.

This Judeo-Christian perspective was reaffirmed
more recently by the late Supreme Court Justice William O. Douglas, who asserted that "we are a religious
people, and our institutions presuppose a Supreme
Being."

In choosing the absolute standard of nature and nature's God as articulated in the Old Testament in general and the Ten Commandments in particular, the
Founders also made the decision to safeguard the
rights of individuals and the minority from the tyr-

anny of an unlimited majority. In choosing the absolute standard of God, they rejected an arbitrary human standard, a standard that changes constantly according to the whim of the majority. They rejected, in essence, a purely democratic form of government.

THE FORM OF OUR GOVERNMENT

The decision to base our system of justice on an absolute standard rather than an arbitrary one also dictated the form of government we now have. As Jefferson stated, we chose to be a nation based on laws rather than men, we also chose to be a constitutional republic, not a democracy.

To understand our choice of a *form* of government, it's essential to differentiate between the double meanings of the word *democracy*. One meaning of the word relates to the *type* of government that features genuinely free elections by the people. The other meaning of the word relates to a *form* of government in which the majority is unlimited, lacking any safeguard to the rights of the individual or the minority.

Confusion frequently exists in this country because we have a democratic *type* of government that features free elections. We are not, however, a democratic *form* of government. In fact, a democracy and a republic are not only dissimilar forms of government, but they are also antithetical. In a constitutional republic, the majority is limited by a written constitution that, so long as it is strictly followed, safeguards the rights of the individual and the minority. In a democratic form of government, there are no such safeguards.

The rights of the majority *and* the minority are safe only so long as we insist on a government that recognizes its most important responsibility to be the one the Framers of the Constitution listed first—to establish and administer justice based on the absolute standards of the "Laws of Nature" and of "Nature's God.

GOD AND THE STATE

Today many confuse their constitutionally guaranteed right to refuse to worship, or even to reject the existence of "Nature's God," with an imagined right that never appears in the Constitution. They insist that the absolute laws of nature and of nature's God, to which Jefferson referred in the Declaration of Independence, be replaced with arbitrary human laws. In fact, the freedom of religion envisioned by the Framers in no way allows any individual such a right. The separation of the institution of civil government from the institutions of the church and synagogue must never be perverted in such a way as to separate the Creator God and His standards of right and wrong from our civil government.

To allow such a separation would be to overthrow the fundamental precept the Founders used to establish our nation—that our liberties come from God and the state therefore may only protect them, not tamper with them or take them away. To allow God to be divorced from our national identity would not only undermine our system of justice, but would also render meaningless the four words presently inscribed above the Speaker's podium located in the chamber of the House of Representatives in the Capitol of the United States. Those four words, "In God We Trust," explain in awesome simplicity why the United States of America has in the past been known throughout the world for its system of justice, and why it has enjoyed such peace and prosperity. The same four words also appear on the face of our coins and paper money. And in the fourth verse of our national anthem, "The Star Spangled Banner," they are asserted to be our national motto.

That the Framers did not at all intend to separate the

Creator from our federal government is evident throughout the voluminous records of their thoughts and proceedings. They clearly did not hold the view of the secularists of our day that the public sector should be divested of any indication, of any representation, which might suggest that we are in fact a religious people, a people who recognize the relevance of God the Creator.

One of the best sources in this regard is Thomas Jefferson, the Founder whom modern secular minds seem to love to quote most. It was Jefferson who penned the words in the Declaration that declared that the unalienable rights of people come from the Creator, and that the state, therefore, may not abolish them. Moreover, in Jefferson's own memorial in Washington, D.C., are carved the following words—a testimony, as it were, for all the nation to see. His words certify where he and his fellow Founders stood on this matter of God and the state as opposed to the *institution* of the church and the institution of the state:

> God who gave us life gave us liberty. Can the liberties of a nation be secure when we have removed their only firm basis, a conviction in the minds of the people that these liberties are the gift of God? That they are not to be violated but with His wrath? Indeed, I tremble for my country when I reflect that God is just: that his Justice cannot sleep forever.

Far from seeing the Creator God as having no bearing whatsoever on the affairs of state, Jefferson saw Him as having the most basic and fundamental bearing of all: He was the source and protector of those liberties the Founders cherished most. According to Jefferson's own words, a belief in God as the source of our liberties is "the only firm basis" of those liberties.

Through the modern separation-of-church-and-state notion, however, what Jefferson feared is actually coming to pass; the conviction that our liberties are from the Creator God is being removed from the minds of our people. In fact, God has virtually been made an illegal subject in that state institution most devoted to the shaping of the minds and values of our people, the public schools. How far we have declined from Jefferson's lofty perspective on the role God must play in the affairs of state!

Even John Kennedy, another president very much admired by the secular minds of our day, felt the need to at least nod in the direction of Jefferson's original conception of the relationship between God and the state. In his famous inaugural address, Kennedy said, "And yet the same revolutionary beliefs for which our forebears fought are still at issue around the globe— the belief that the rights of man come not from the generosity of the state, but from the hand of God."

My hope is that we will recapture this conception, not just the memory of the words, but also their meaning. We must again peg our liberties firmly in a full-blown conception of a Creator God. We must stress again with our children that the freedoms enshrined in our Declaration and Constitution were viewed by the Founders as coming from Him, and that He ordained civil government as the instrument of His protection for those rights.

That such a perspective should sound so foreign and controversial to people today is a tragic and striking sign of how far we are removed from the thinking of our colonial fathers. Given the current intellectual climate, it is hard to imagine a public school teacher or college professor stressing to students how our liberties have come from God and that we must not remove Him from the minds of our people. But we desperately need to recover that very perspective lest we forfeit the priceless system of justice and personal liberties the Founding Fathers bequeathed to us.

3

Symptom: A Failure to Protect Life

*I*ronically, as the federal government has assumed more and more responsibilities never granted to it by the people in their Constitution, it has failed to meet the most fundamental responsibility placed on it by the Constitution, the responsibility of protecting life and liberty. Whenever the federal government fails in the area of meeting such a fundamental responsibility, a constitutional crisis necessarily follows.

Such was the case when our ancestors stood silent as thousands of black Americans were deprived of their freedom in the name of legalized slavery. It was this constitutional crisis that inspired Abraham Lincoln to make the statement to which I previously referred.

Lincoln understood that the federal government's constitutional responsibility to protect the life and liberty of every American is the very essence of our form of government. He also understood that its continued failure to meet its responsibility jeopardized the very survival of our constitutional republic.

In Lincoln's day, our Constitution had been rendered meaningless by the judges and lawmakers who chose to accommodate the social and economic pressures of their time rather than uphold the absolute principles that had been set forth in the Declaration and upon which our Constitution had been founded.

SLAVERY AND THE CONSTITUTION

This constitutional crisis occurred because, although the Founders incorporated the principles of life and liberty into our Constitution, they did not adequately work out the implications of those principles with respect to black slaves. In defense of the Founders, it must be said that given the tenor of the times, they were fortunate to even create and gain acceptance for a new federal government that provided for the people to govern themselves. That was a tall order in and of itself. To obtain a Constitution, a majority of the Founders decided it best that the issue of slavery remain to be dealt with by another generation that would have the benefit of living under the stable order the Founders created.

With the exception of three brief and rather oblique references to slavery in the context of prohibiting the importation of slaves after 1808, recognizing the property rights of slave owners, and requiring slaves to be counted as three-fifths of a person for purpose of a state's representation in the House of Representatives, the Constitution, even with the Bill of Rights, made no reference whatsoever to the practice of slavery. It did not address the subject further because those who opposed slavery feared that any attempt to deal with the subject would preclude any sort of constitution from being accepted by the Constitutional Convention, much less being ratified by the requisite number of states.

The failure of the Constitution to deal with this divisive issue nearly destroyed our republic seventy years later. Though slavery had been condoned and accommodated since the inception of our republic, the crisis that had been brewing since the first slaves were brought to American shores came to a head in 1857.

The Dred Scott Decision

In 1857, the Supreme Court in the *Dred Scott* case held that blacks were entitled to none of the rights described so eloquently in the Declaration of Independence, the same rights subsequently guaranteed to every other American by the Constitution. The reason for the justices' decision was very simple. Rather than establishing and administering the standard of justice on which our system was based, the Court chose instead to accommodate the will of the politically and economically powerful.

The *Dred Scott* case arose as the result of a number of individuals who took our Constitution and the rights guaranteed by it seriously. The suit was brought because Dred Scott, a slave, and those who opposed the institution of slavery knew that if we were to allow the fundamental and unalienable right to liberty to be denied to certain individuals by a political compromise, both our Constitution and all the rights it was written to protect would be meaningless. They understood the significance of the Founders' conclusion that life and liberty were rights that God and God alone could give and take.

Lawmakers and judges are great at compromising, and that's what the *Dred Scott* case was all about. It had its roots in a political compromise known as the "Missouri Compromise," adopted by Congress in 1820, which stated that blacks were at the same time both persons and property, depending on where they happened to find themselves geographically. Anywhere below a certain arbitrarily drawn line they were to be considered property, and anywhere above that same line they were to be considered persons.

Scott's lawyers pointed out in their argument to the justices of the Supreme Court that blacks cannot at the same time be both persons and property; either they are persons or they are property. They argued that barring overwhelming evidence to the contrary, there must be a presumption that blacks are persons. They further pointed out that although both the Declaration of Independence and the Constitution guarantee to all the right to life and liberty, the institution of slavery made such a guarantee meaningless.

Chief Justice Taney, speaking for the majority, addressed this argument as it relates to the Constitution as follows:

The words "people of the United States" and "citizens" are synonymous terms, and mean the same thing. They both describe the political body who, according to our republican institutions, form the sovereignty, and who hold the power and conduct the Government through their representatives. They are what we familiarly call the "sovereign people," and every citizen is one of this people, and a constituent member of this sovereignty. The question before us is, whether the class of persons described in the plea in abatement compose a portion of this people, and are constituent members of this sovereignty? We think they are not, and that they are not included, and were not intended to be included, under the word "citizens" in the Constitution, and can therefore claim none of the rights and privileges which that instrument provides for and secures to citizens of the United States. On the contrary, they were at that time considered as a subordinate and inferior class of beings, who had been subjugated by the dominant race, and, whether emancipated or not, yet remained subject to their authority, and had no rights or privileges but such as those who held the power and the Government might choose to grant them.

It is not the province of the court to decide upon the justice or injustice, the policy or impolicy, or these laws.

With regard to the words of the Declaration of Independence, Chief Justice Taney, later in the same decision, responded:

The language of the Declaration of Independence is equally conclusive:

It begins by declaring that, "when in the course of human events it becomes necessary for one people to dissolve the political bands which have connected them with another, and to assume among the powers of the earth the separate and equal station to which the laws of nature and nature's God entitle them, a decent respect for the opinions of mankind requires that they should declare the causes which impel them to the separation."

It then proceeds to say: "We hold these truths to be self-evident: that all men are created equal; that they are endowed by their Creator with certain unalienable rights; that among these are life, liberty, and the pursuit of happiness; that to secure these rights, Governments are instituted, deriving their just powers from the consent of the governed."

The general words above quoted would seem to embrace the whole human family, and if they were used in a similar instrument at this day would be so understood. But it is too clear for dispute, that the enslaved African race were not intended to be included, and formed no part of the people who framed and adopted this declaration; for if the language, as understood in that day, would embrace them, the conduct of the distinguished men who framed the Declaration of Independence would have been utterly and flagrantly inconsistent with the principles they asserted; and instead of the sympathy of mankind, to which they so confidently appealed, they would have deserved and received universal rebuke and reprobation.[1]

The Supreme Court resolved the explosive conflict between the economic interest of slaveowners and the rights of *all* persons to life and liberty by simply declaring that blacks were not persons but property and, consequently, weren't entitled to any constitutional rights. With one fell swoop of the pen, seven of the nine justices of the Supreme Court established the legal status, and plight, of thousands of slaves in our country.

After the Supreme Court ruling in the *Dred Scott* case, the principles that had set this nation apart were officially and practically meaningless. Rather than the federal government's protecting the God-given right to liberty, it was actually condoning its deprivation.

Lincoln's Moral Leadership

Fortunately for our republic, individuals like Abraham Lincoln had the courage to take a moral stand, even though such a stand was at the time unpopular and politically dangerous. Had polling data been available, it undoubtedly would have shown his position on the issue to be in a clear minority. In the wake of the *Dred Scott* decision, Lincoln and others who shared his conviction that right was right, even when the majority and man's law were wrong, decided to focus their attack at the heart of the issue. Were we as a nation to continue to embrace the God-centered world view the Founding Fathers had chosen to embrace? Were we to continue to embrace a world view recognizing that God created people with the right to life and liberty and subsequently established civil government to protect those rights? Or were we now to reject that world view for a man-centered philosophy, a world view in which the majority determines what is right, even if that determination is in direct conflict with the laws of nature?

In essence, Lincoln was saying that just because something is legal doesn't necessarily make it right. He was arguing in favor of what the writers of the Declaration called "the law of Nature's God." He was saying that to be legitimate, legislation passed by the majority must conform to natural law, because natural law supersedes man's law. Lincoln agreed with the view expressed by George Mason, one of the most influential of our Founders, who had said, "The laws of nature are the laws of God, whose authority can be superseded by no power on earth."[2]

To put what Lincoln and Mason were saying into perspective, imagine for a moment that tomorrow Congress were to pass a resolution that says, "Effective next July 1, the United States will no longer recognize the law of gravity." We all know that next July 1, regardless of whether we choose to recognize it, the law of gravity would continue to govern. If we were to walk outside on July 1, the natural law of gravity would still cause any object thrown into the air to fall to the ground, despite our new law to the contrary. Lincoln was saying the same thing more than 100 years ago. He was saying that you can make slavery legal, but the fact that it's legal does not change the more fundamental truth that it's still morally wrong.

Although his opposition to the Supreme Court's decision in the *Dred Scott* case cost him the general election in his Senate race in November 1858, Lincoln eventually prevailed politically and morally. Two years later he was elected president of the United States. More importantly, he was elected president without compromising his position that slavery would not be allowed to be extended into any new territories or states. As one of his final acts as president, he prevailed even further. By signing the Emancipation Proclamation, he not only accomplished his original objective of preventing the further spread of slavery, but also succeeded in totally abolishing it. To achieve his objective, Lincoln, without ever compromising his principles, negotiated, one step at a time, until he achieved his ultimate objective in its entirety.

We now recognize Lincoln's fortitude in withstanding the social and economic pressures of his time. Had it not been for him, our Constitution may well have been an extinct document today, useful only to students of history. Had we allowed the *Dred Scott* decision to stand, our Constitution, for all intents and purposes, would have failed.

THE PARALLEL
WITH ABORTION

It's interesting to me that we can now look back at slavery as a shameful chapter in our country's history and at the same time be blind to the fact that today, barely more than 100 years later, we are repeating exactly the same error. This time the victims of our error are the unborn, the parents of the unborn, and the couples in America who are willing to wait as long as ten years to adopt an infant child.

Polls taken in our country today indicate that many Americans are opposed to the federal government's involvement in the issue of abortion in any way, even if such a position has the effect of condoning the practice. Their argument of convenience ignores the fact that just as the federal government was involved in the issue of slavery when it condoned the practice for seventy years, it is equally involved now when it condones the practice of abortion.

Because the federal government is charged with the constitutional responsibility of protecting human life, it fails when it condones the taking of innocent life, notwithstanding its claim of neutrality. Let's remember it was federal neutrality that allowed the practice of slavery. Further, it was federal involvement, the Supreme Court's decision in *Roe* v. *Wade* in 1973 to be exact, that allowed the legalization of abortion in the first place.

The arguments made today to justify the federal government's condoning abortion are not unlike the arguments made by those who defended the federal government's condoning of slavery. Many have drawn the striking parallels between slavery and abortion— justifiably, in my estimation.

"Personally Opposed"?

Today many say they are personally opposed to abortion but don't think that it's their right to impose their views on others. They argue that individuals ought to have the right to make their own choices. Such an argument sounds a lot like what the abolitionists heard people say. I'm sure many were personally opposed to slavery but didn't feel it was their right to impose their view on others. They undoubtably felt slave owners ought to decide for themselves whether it was right to own slaves. The federal government, they argued, had no right to interfere with those slave owners' freedom of choice. But what about the rights of the slaves?

A Hierarchy of Values

The problem with the argument made by those in favor of slavery was that it failed to recognize that different individual rights must be placed in a hierarchy of rights, an ascending scale of values wherein we may see which individual rights are more important than others, and which ones must give way when there's a conflict. The law that requires us to stop at red lights is a necessary law, but it must give way to the higher law of saving human life when an ambulance is speeding to a hospital with a dying patient. Ambulances may go through red lights, speed, drive on the wrong side of the road, and so on because preserving human life is at the absolute top of our hierarchy of values. The slavery generation failed to deal correctly with the inevitable problem presented when the rights of different individuals conflict with one another. Similarly, our generation has failed to deal correctly with the same exact issue.

The rights guaranteed by the Constitution are rights that necessarily will, at times, find themselves in conflict. For example, my First Amendment right to free speech is not without limitations. What happens when my right to free speech conflicts with someone else's right not to hear my speech? If I were to stand outside someone's home tonight with a megaphone, delivering a speech that would be fully protected if given on the floor of the House of Representatives, wouldn't that person in front of whose house I was speaking most likely call the police and say, "There's some clown outside my window using a megaphone, exercising his First Amendment right to free speech. What about my right to be able to sleep at night?" Undoubtedly, my right to free speech would come to an abrupt halt when the paddy wagon arrived. The reason is that my freedom of speech under those circumstances is inferior to another person's right to enjoy his or her property without disturbance.

Similarly, despite the First Amendment right to free speech, laws exist that make it illegal for anyone to scream "fire" in a crowded theater when the individual knows that no such fire or threat of fire exists.

Our Constitution has worked so well, in large part, because it recognizes this hierarchy of individual rights and freedoms. Under our Constitution, some rights by definition are superior to others.

ABORTION: DENIAL OF THE FIRST RIGHT, LIFE

According to our Declaration of Independence and Constitution, no rights are more fundamental or of higher priority than the rights to life and liberty, in that order. While this principle now appears to be clear when discussed in the context of an issue like slavery, it is not so clear when discussed in the context of a more contemporary issue like abortion. As they say, hindsight is always 20–20. Every generation seems to see clearly the mistakes of previous generations while being blind to its own, often more-grievous, mistakes.

Since 1973, more than 1.5 million children have died each year because the Supreme Court, in the historic and tragic *Roe* v. *Wade* case, declared the right of a mother to let a doctor destroy her unborn child through abortion. The number of children who have died as a result of abortion *each year* is now greater than the combined fatalities of American soldiers in the Revolutionary War, the War Between the States, World War I, World War II, the Korean Conflict, and Vietnam. We have now destroyed through abortion a population equivalent in size to the nation of Canada. In fact, in America today, abortion claims the life of a baby every seventeen seconds. That's 4,500 a day. In many of our cities, there are more abortions each year than live births. In one hospital in northern Virginia, almost 15 percent of the abortions are in the sixth month of pregnancy. Ninety-seven percent of the abortions are for the convenience of the mother. It's not uncommon for parents to abort a child because the child is the "wrong" sex.

The Babies Who Survived

Though most of the children who have been aborted have been killed by the procedure, some have survived the abortion, only to then be intentionally allowed to die outside the womb. There were, for example, at least fourteen such live births in 1983 in the city of Atlanta.

I learned of these live births because one lady meticulously sifted through the records of live births and deaths in the state of Georgia Bureau of Vital Statistics. She was able to document these live births and subsequent deaths because the state requires a certificate for every live birth even if the child is not allowed to live. By matching death certificates to birth certificates, she documented these live births that resulted because the abortion procedures "failed to work." In other words, the babies survived the saline solution and maiming; the attempts to kill them were botched, and they survived, at least for a while.

Because the purpose of the abortion procedures was to kill rather than give birth to the children, no measures were taken after the abortion to save the fragile lives of the burned and maimed children. Predictably, each of the fourteen children died shortly after their births, and no charges were pressed against any of those responsible for the deaths. I mention this story because too many people think that abortions have nothing to do with children, only "fetuses," a clinical term that attempts through euphemism to conceal the grisly reality of the death and dismemberment of a baby boy or girl.

THE COURT'S FLAWED LOGIC

In the *Roe* v. *Wade* decision legalizing abortion, the Supreme Court relied on the same flawed logic its predecessor had used in 1857 to condone slavery.

Just as it had done in the *Dred Scott* decision, the Supreme Court in the *Roe* v. *Wade* case, in a seven-to-two split decision, held abortion to be constitutional by simply saying that unborn children are not persons within the meaning of the Fifth Amendement. This is significant, because the Fifth Amendment states that "no person shall be deprived of life . . . without due process of law."

Once it is determined that personhood is a subjective question—that is, personhood may be conferred or withheld by judicial discretion—and that the right to life is equally subjective, then the principle that the right to life and the right to liberty are unalienable is meaningless, as are the safeguards that are written into our Constitution to protect those rights.

The Founders held that our rights were given by God and that the state could not justifiably take them away without due process of law. This is, as previously pointed out, the perspective of the God-centered world view on which our institutions are based. In *Roe* v. *Wade,* we have seen the expression of the man-centered world view, which says that our rights, even the right to life, may be removed by governmental action, in this case a court decision.

Presumption of Innocence?

One of the most significant aspects of the abortion issue was totally ignored by the Supreme Court in its 1973 decision, as well as in subsequent decisions relating to abortion. Namely, in our system of justice there supposedly exists a presumption in favor of innocence when considering whether someone has committed a punishable offense. In the case of the unborn, the presumption ought to be in favor of personhood and life rather than nonhumanity and death, unless and until conclusive proof to the contrary is presented. Such proof is to be presented and conviction or innocence determined by due process of law. In the case of abortion, there has been no such proof and no due process of law. There has only been a presumption of guilt and immediate execution, where the mother and physician serve as judges, jury, and executioners.

Consider for a moment, by way of analogy, the absurdity of the Court's presumption that the unborn are not persons. Assume that you are sitting in your living room and hear a loud screeching of tires outside. You discover that there was an automobile accident in which an individual has been severely injured, and at least superficially, that individual *appears* to be dead. Surely there is not a rational person who would immediately say, "Call the hearse and have that person buried." Any rational person would instead say, "Let's check the person's vital signs. Let's make absolutely certain before we call a hearse rather than ambulance that the person is in fact dead."

Certainly such a precautionary measure is rational. Yet when it comes to the issue of abortion, somehow we have failed to apply that same test. We had not debated or settled the question of whether the unborn child is fully human and alive at the time the Court made its fatal decision. Today we continue to close our eyes to the reality of what abortion is all about.

To use another popular analogy, when hunters are in the woods they are not supposed to shoot at just anything that moves, or at any and all movement in the woods. The reason is obvious—what's moving may be another hunter! Those who have gone ahead and blasted away at any movement have ended up killing dogs, cows, horses, and even their fellow hunters. The folly of shooting first and asking questions later in such circumstances is evident.

But that is precisely what we've done with abortion. We've blasted away before finding out more about what we're destroying, before coming to a settled, well-thought-out conclusion about the life and personhood of the little boys and girls we are crushing, beheading, burning, and otherwise mangling as we torturously execute them through abortions. One might say that the *Roe* v. *Wade* decision is to our generation what the *Dred Scott* decision was to Lincoln's generation. It is a Supreme Court decision that allows us to avoid dealing with the issue of abortion openly and responsibly. By hiding behind the Supreme Court and blaming them for the legalization of abortion, we apparently think we can wash our generation's hands of any responsibility or culpability for the deaths of more than twenty million unborn children in the last fourteen years.

DOES MANNER OF CONCEPTION MATTER?

Interestingly enough, we have also come to believe that the circumstances under which a child is conceived are relevant to the issue of the legality of abortion. When I was running for reelection to Congress in 1986, an Atlanta newspaper reporter interviewed me on a wide range of issues. One of her questions went something like this: "I understand that you are opposed to abortion."

"That's correct," I replied.

She then asked, "Certainly you're not opposed to abortion under the circumstances of rape and incest, are you?"

My response seemed to surprise her: "Because I don't think the circumstances under which a child is conceived are relevant to the issue, I would not favor abortion in the case of rape and incest. The only relevant issue is whether or not the unborn are persons entitled to the right to continue living." I then explained my answer to her. "If you really believe that the circumstances under which a child is conceived are relevant, I would presume that you would agree with me that someone could go anywhere in the country today and kill any child whom that person could prove beyond a reasonable doubt was conceived in rape or incest. Under your line of reasoning, someone would be justified in killing the child, and such a killing would be condoned under the law."

She instantly replied, "That's absurd."

"Why is that absurd?" I asked.

"Because in the case you just mentioned, the child is alive," she responded.

Having heard her response before, I immediately replied, "You have just conceded, then, that the circumstances under which a child is conceived are irrelevant. The only relevant question is the question of whether the child is a human being, not under what circumstances the child became a human being."

The Founders were very clear about when human life begins for purposes of establishing when the unalienable rights to life and liberty attach, and when the responsibility of civil government to protect those rights begins. In the Declaration of Independence, the Founders expressly stated that "all men are *created* equal." Notice that they didn't say we are "born" equal; they said we are "created" equal. The unalienable rights to which they referred attach from the moment of creation, not from the moment of birth, as those who favor abortion have rewritten the Declaration and Constitution to suggest.

Why do we use two standards when we deal with the abortion issue, one standard when the child is outside the womb, another standard when the child is inside the womb? Inside the womb the child is fair game for brutal abortion procedures, while outside the womb the child is entitled to the full protection of the law. That's about as logical as saying that blacks are people in certain states, but mere property in other states.

I continued my interview with the reporter by telling a personal story. A friend of mine recently related his experience with his daughter, who gave birth to a child that was three months premature. My friend was moved by the fact that, following the birth of his grandson, his daughter went each night to the hospital to hold his grandson in the incubator. She did this for weeks.

Months later he confided in me, "You know, that experience changed my entire perspective on abortion. Suddenly I realized that the child was capable of living outside the mother's womb, and yet that was the same time frame in which, under our laws, a mother could have legally taken that child's life."

WHAT ABOUT THE LIFE OF THE MOTHER?

After hearing the story about my friend's experience, the reporter, in a somewhat mellowed tone, asked, "Well, what about the life of the mother? Surely, you would agree that when the life of the mother is in jeopardy, abortion ought to be legal."

I responded by explaining that under those circumstances, abortion has always been legal because it is self-defense, and because it is better to save one life than lose both. If the child is too premature to live outside the mother's womb, yet its continued struggle for life threatens the mother's physical life, then clearly because both lives will be lost it is better to save at least the mother than to risk losing her, too. The child will die in either case.

Clearly abortion is and always has been legal to save the physical life of the mother. However, this involves less than 1 percent of all abortions in the country. In fact, the *combined* incidents of abortions relating to rape, incest, or a situation threatening the life of the mother account for less than 1 percent of all abortions performed in America today, and they should therefore by no means be used to justify the wholesale, elective abortion policy we now follow. The overwhelming majority of elective abortions are performed as a method of postconceptual birth control.

As can be seen easily by my interview with the Atlanta newspaper reporter, we in this country somehow are too seldom interested in how we reach our conclusions. Too frequently we are only interested in knowing the bottom-line answer. Are you prolife or are you prochoice? Are you for or against prayer in school? Our answers to such questions ought to be based on thoughtful and full consideration of the entire issue. How we reach our conclusions on issues as complex and important as abortion can be as important as the conclusions themselves.

UNWANTED CHILDREN DO NOT EXIST

Another irrelevant and illogical argument frequently made to justify abortion is that the unborn child is unwanted. Aside from the simple fact that whether or not a person is wanted should never be relevant in determining the legality of the taking of innocent life, there's another glaring flaw in this argument. It never states *by whom* the supposedly unwanted child is unwanted. The unborn child may well be unwanted by the natural parents, but that certainly doesn't mean the child is unwanted by anyone else. Such an argument totally ignores the fact that in many areas of the country, there is currently a ten-year waiting list for parents who desire to adopt infant children. Accordingly, it's totally misleading and dishonest to attempt to justify abortion on the grounds that the child is unwanted.

Mother—The Other Victim

Perhaps the greatest tragedy of abortion is that aside from the parents who can't have children of their own and would give anything to adopt an infant child, each abortion has at least two other victims. One victim obviously is the child who is without any recourse, legal or otherwise. The other victim is the natural mother.

We are now learning that there are deep emotional scars caused by an abortion. Frequently, expectant mothers are advised to get an abortion so as to avoid a career interruption, or, in the case of an unwed mother, to avoid public embarrassment. Seldom, however, do future mothers receive advice that includes any assessment of the emotional damage inflicted by the experience. Once the deed is done, many young women find the guilt and remorse overwhelming and require long-term help in coming to terms with it.

SUPREME COURT DECISIONS: THE LAST WORD?

One final point needs to be made regarding the issue of abortion and the propriety of the Supreme Court in resolving it. This point was made very succintly and persuasively by Abraham Lincoln when he addressed the issue of slavery in his first inaugural address.

I do not forget the position assumed by some that constitutional questions are to be decided by the Supreme Court, nor do I deny that such decisions must be binding in any case upon the parties to a suit as to the object of that suit, while they are also entitled to very high respect and consideration in all parallel cases by all other departments of the Government. And while it is obviously possible that such decision may be erroneous in any given case, still the evil effect following it, being limited to that particular case, with the chance that it may be overruled and never become a precedent for other cases, can better be borne than could the evils of a different practice. At the same time, the candid citizen must confess that if the policy of the Government upon vital questions affecting the whole people is to be irrevocably fixed by decisions of the Supreme Court, the instant they are made in ordinary litigation between parties in personal actions the people will have ceased to be their own rulers, having to that extent practically resigned their Government into the hands of that eminent tribunal. . . .

This country, with its institutions, belongs to the people who inhabit it. Whenever they shall grow weary of the existing Government, they can exercise their constitutional right of amending it or their revolutionary right to dismember or overthrow it. I can not be ignorant of the fact that many worthy and patriotic citizens are desirous of having the National Constitution amended. While I make no recommendation of amendments, I fully recognize the rightful authority of the people over the whole subject, to be exercised in either of the modes prescribed in the instrument itself; and I should, under existing circumstances, favor rather than oppose a fair opportunity being afforded to people to act upon it.[3]

Today, there are those who argue that the *Roe* v. *Wade* decision has resolved the issue of abortion once and for all. The Supreme Court has spoken, and that's it. But President Lincoln gave sound advice here. The government is of the people and by the people, not of and by that "eminent tribunal," the Supreme Court. If the Court has the final word, the people will indeed have "ceased to be their own rulers." Fortunately, the Constitution provides for amendments and constitutional conventions, which are fully legal and proper measures but which advocates of the Court's recent rulings curiously dread.

Need for an Amendment

Many of the same individuals who support the legalization of abortion on demand argue against the consideration of a constitutional amendment reversing the *Roe* v. *Wade* decision. However, since any effort by the Congress to legislatively reverse that decision would be held unconstitutional by the Supreme Court, a constitutional amendment is the *only* avenue available to address this important issue. To date, the House of Representatives has never once even considered, much less debated, such an amendment on the floor of the House.

The hypocrisy of the argument made by those who refuse to allow such a debate on the grounds that the Supreme Court has spoken, and that the Court is the final word, can best be seen by turning the tables around. Ask any who advocate the propriety of the Supreme Court's being the ultimate authority on this issue if they would hold to the same opinion were the composition of the Supreme Court to change in such a way that the Court itself reverses the *Roe* v. *Wade* decision. Such individuals almost always concede that under those circumstances they would be among the first to argue for a constitutional amendment.

These individuals may soon have the opportunity to reassess their position. With the recent resignation of Justice Lewis Powell, the current Supreme Court may well soon reverse the *Roe* v. *Wade* holding. Regardless of where an individual stands on the abortion issue, however, it is too important to be decided by that "eminent tribunal" alone; it's an issue on which the people themselves must deliberate and decide.

INFANTICIDE AND EUTHANASIA

The sanctity of life issue goes well beyond the question of abortion. It affects every aspect of life, including how our society treats our infants after birth and our elderly. In this connection, I can still vividly recall hearing the late theologian Dr. Francis Schaeffer state in 1972, the year before the *Roe* v. *Wade* decision, that if America ever devalues human life by legalizing abortion, infanticide and euthanasia will certainly follow.

Regrettably, Dr. Schaeffer's words were prophetic. Infanticide and euthanasia are no longer unthinkable. For example, in 1984 the 98th Congress passed S540, which contained a provision specifying that National-Institute-of-Health(NIH)-funded research using human fetuses may be conducted on nonviable, living human fetuses outside the womb to develop important biomedical information that could not otherwise be obtained and that did not increase the risk of suffering or injury or death to the fetus. For fetuses in the womb, the research must enhance the well-being of the fetus and present only minimal risk, whether the fetus is intended for abortion or is to be carried to term. But for President Reagan's veto, S540 would have become law.

Not too long ago newspapers attributed a statement to Colorado Governor Richard Lamm that suggested our elderly have an obligation to die because they have become a liability rather than an asset. From a utilitarian perspective in which human life is measured exclusively by its ability to produce, this suggestion is both logical and inevitable. Today, our society as a whole has reached a point where the value of life is measured by such utilitarian standards. How else can we explain the current debate over whether parents should have the right to end the life of a physically handicapped child so long as the decision is made within the first several days following birth and so long as the attending physician concurs?

Elderly Abuse

Once the right to life is determined by such utilitarian and subjective standards, child abuse and abuse of the elderly are certain to increase. Unfortunately, we as a nation do not seem to see the connection between our attitudes regarding abortion and our attitudes toward our children and our elderly. Doesn't it seem logical that a society that will allow the abortion of defenseless, innocent, unborn children will eventually abuse other equally defenseless and innocent children and the elderly? Are the number of abortions and the increasing number of newborn infants being left in trash containers to die unrelated?

Our unwillingness to make the connection between elderly abuse and our basic devaluation of human life became crystal clear to me during a recent hearing of the House Select Committee on Aging. The hearing was designed to focus on the recent increase of elderly abuse in America. Actor Kirk Douglas testified before the Committee because he had recently played the role of an elderly man who was abused in a nursing home. (For actors to testify before House committees because of their experience in portraying certain roles ranging from farmers' wives to war veterans is a recent trend that appears to be on the increase.)

After stating his concerns about elderly abuse, Douglas yielded to the members of the committee for questions. The following excerpt from the hearing transcript demonstrates our society's unwillingness to accept the validity of the connection between the devaluation of human life in general and elderly abuse or child abuse in particular.

> *Mr. Swindall:* Mr. Douglas, first of all, I want to commend you for your testimony, and I certainly concur with everything that you said. But I would like to ask you a more general question, and that is, do you not think that, at least in part, the problem of the ever-increasing incidence of abuse of our Nation's elderly might well be linked to our society's devaluing of human life in general, which has resulted in the wake of the historic *Roe v. Wade* decision, which basically legalized abortion in this country?

> *Mr. Douglas:* I am not going to get involved in that. Everybody has their own personal evaluations. Abortion is an entirely different issue that

right now is a very hot issue. People are very strongly convinced on both sides, but one issue that I think can be a unanimity of opinion has to do with elderly abuse.

Mr. Swindall: But, is there not a common linkage between the two issues, and that is the value which this society places on human life?

Mr. Douglas: I do not see that commonly.

CAPITAL PUNISHMENT

Many today believe that it is inconsistent to oppose abortion and at the same time advocate capital punishment. To believe these two positions to be inconsistent, however, reflects a fundamental lack of understanding regarding why human life is special and why civil government has the responsibility to protect it.

As our Founders declared, it is because God created human life in His own image, and created civil government to protect it, that two conclusions follow. The first conclusion is that abortion is morally wrong because it is the taking of innocent human life created in God's image. The second conclusion is that capital punishment by civil government, not by aggrieved friends or relatives, is sanctioned because an innocent human life created in the image of God was wrongly taken.

Abortion is wrong because human life is sacred. Capital punishment exists because human life is sacred. In the book of Genesis, chapter 9, verse 6, this principle is clearly stated: "Whoso sheddeth man's blood, by man shall his blood be shed: for in the image of God made he man."

Because human life is distinct from any other form of life, it cannot be taken by anyone except civil government as God's designated agent. And even then, human life is to be taken only in certain instances and only after satisfying clear conditions designed to safeguard against the unjust taking of an innocent human life. Thus, it is because human life is so special that anyone who takes an innocent life should have his or her life taken, not by an aggrieved friend or relative in revenge, but by the civil government after due process of law. A failure by civil government to protect innocent human life will eventually lead to individuals' taking the law into their own hands, as was the case with Bernard Goetz in the recent New York subway shooting case.

While the concept of capital punishment is valid and consistent with a prolife or antiabortion viewpoint, it's important to note that our judicial system has failed in its responsibility regarding capital punishment in two very specific ways. First, it has not consistently and expeditiously applied capital punishment. Second, it has not applied it equally. Despite a recent Supreme Court case minimizing the significance of statistical evidence, it is an indictment against our current system of justice that statistics have shown that the probability of receiving the death penalty is significantly greater if the defendant is indigent, black, or hispanic than if wealthy and white.

The solution to this problem, however, is not to eliminate capital punishment but to apply it equally, consistently, and expeditiously to all who take innocent life by premeditation. Whether the issue is abortion or capital punishment, the principle is the same. A belief in the sanctity of human life requires the civil government to protect innocent human life from those who would take it by abortion or by any other premeditated means. To oppose abortion except in the case of self-defense and to support capital punishment except in the case of self-defense, or where premeditation is lacking, are consistent pro-life positions.

Similarly, to support abortion and to oppose capital punishment are positions consistent with a world view that holds that there is nothing sacred about human life. Stated differently, a man-centered, utilitarian world view allows an individual to justify fetal experimentation, euthanasia and abortion because human beings, aside from their ability to rationalize what they selfishly desire to achieve or do, are no different from any other life form.

Both capital punishment and opposition to abortion, on the other hand, are the result of the God-centered world view of our Founders.

CONCLUSION

The integrity of our constitutional republic rests ultimately on how we resolve the life-and-death issues of abortion and capital punishment. If we are unable to preserve the most fundamental rights of which our Constitution speaks, life and liberty, our government has failed to satisfy its most basic responsibility. Such a government not only forfeits the respect of the people, but eventually its right and ability to govern as well.

4

Symptom: Our National Debt and Continuing Annual Deficits

*A*side from the very important decision to base our system of justice on the absolute standards of nature's God, the Founders made another, equally important decision. Consistent with their God-centered world view, they also decided to separate the responsibilities of civil government from those of other institutions. They recognized that in the overall scheme of things, there are numerous institutions or governments, each with very specific realms of responsibility. In addition to the institution of civil government in general and the federal, state, and local governments in particular, they recognized the existence and responsibilities of other institutions including the family, church (which would include synagogues, temples, and other religious institutions), private associations, and businesses.

In the preamble of the Constitution and in the Tenth Amendment, the Founders stated their intention to limit the responsibilities of this newly formed central government to the establishment and administration of justice and to fulfilling those other responsibilities expressly enumerated in the Constitution. From that starting point, they wrote a document that has stood the test of time.

Under our Constitution, civil government is to establish and maintain law and order. Institutions and governments other than the federal government are to assume the responsibilities not expressly granted to the federal government. These responsibilities include such things as educating our children and providing assistance to the needy. Simply stated, the wisdom of the Constitution rests in its requirement that unless individuals or local and state governments are, for some specific and compelling reason, ill-equipped or incapable of assuming a particular responsibility, that responsibility is not automatically to be assumed by the federal government.

This was the obvious rationale in the case of each of the responsibilities expressly granted by the people to the federal government in our Constitution. Under the Articles of Confederation, the people had learned that it was impractical, if not impossible, for the various states to provide for an effective national defense, or to regulate commerce between the various states.

Even though the Constitution has never been amended to change these original divisions of responsibilities, we have nevertheless been ignoring them. Consequently, over the past 200 years, we have gradually and unwittingly been changing our Constitution. We have done so to the point that today the federal government is spending billions of dollars in areas where it has no constitutional authority. In the process, it has gradually usurped the responsibilities vested by the Constitution in individuals, in state and local governments, as well as in other institutions.

THE U.S. CONSTITUTION: A BLUEPRINT

There are profound consequences to ignoring the clear delineation of responsibilities contained in our Constitution. Certainly the most obvious consequence is the financial one, including a national debt of unprecedented size and annual federal deficits of equally enormous proportions. But as we shall see in later chapters, there are other, less obvious yet equally significant consequences such as a growing welfare state, mediocrity in public education, and a declining national moral fiber. These consequences have occurred because our Constitution is much more than a document; it is actually a finely drawn and carefully calculated blueprint.

Certainly it would be foolish to build a house without first drawing up a blueprint and following the foundational and structural design set forth in it. It would be equally foolish to build something as complex as a nation without first drawing up and then following a blueprint. Furthermore, just as it would be foolish when building a house to change or ignore a blueprint without first assessing the structural consequences of such a decision, so, too, it would be foolish to make major changes in our Constitution without first calculating whether the foundational documents can accommodate such changes.

Until my wife and I built our own home, I never fully understood the significance of a blueprint. After the foundation had been poured, the frame had been built, and most of the plumbing and electrical wiring had been completed, my wife and I decided that we wanted to add ten feet to our upstairs master bedroom. When I told our builder what we had decided, he responded by simply saying, "It can't be done."

I said, "What do you mean it can't be done? Anything can be done."

"Well, sure, it can be done," he explained. "But I really don't think you'll want to do it, because it would require tearing down almost all the work that has already been completed. The foundation and frame were never designed to accommodate an additional ten feet in your bedroom. To accomplish the change you're suggesting would cost more than double what you've already spent. And once it's completed, I'm not sure I can guarantee the results, because the overall house design is inadequate to accommodate the additional ten feet you're now proposing."

After hearing my builder's explanation, we decided not to add the ten feet for two very good reasons. First, we couldn't afford it, and second, even if we had been able to afford it, it was apparent that the final results would be disastrous.

The same is true when it comes to making changes in our Constitution, even if such changes appear at first blush to be simple and inconsequential. Our constitutional blueprint prescribes a foundation of a particular shape, and it was upon this foundation that our governmental framework is built. It's a framework that suits its foundation.

Now, with the foundation in place and the framework substantially complete, we have been making changes, some major and some minor, that are contrary to the basic design of the foundation. Because we haven't taken the time to study the potential adverse results of our changes in the blueprint, we are unintentionally but just as certainly weakening our entire national structure. The weakening is now so substantial that our whole national edifice, public and private sectors included, is threatened.

DEFICIT, DEBT AND THE BUDGET

Nowhere is the evidence of our potential structural collapse more evident than in our national debt, which now exceeds $2 trillion and is expanding at an annual rate of more than $150 billion. As much as we talk about the federal debt and annual deficits, they are not the real problems. They are merely symptoms of the real problem. The real problem is that we have ignored our constitutional blueprint and have expanded the responsibilities of our federal government far beyond its foundational capacity. We have been trying to erect a castle on a foundation laid for a tract house!

To put it another way, the Founders laid a constitutional foundation shaped by the belief that our federal government would govern best when it governs least. But we have sought to erect on their sound foundation a governmental framework that more suits the belief that our federal government governs best when it governs *most*.

It's important that we understand that the deficit is a symptom of our reversal of our Founders' belief regarding the role of the federal government. Failure to correctly identify the cause of our continuing deficits is as dangerous as misdiagnosing a disease. Our failure to identify the real problem will inevitably lead us to incorrect and possibly harmful remedies, for the same reasons that misdiagnosing a disease or treating it only symptomatically will increase the possibility of prescribing a wrong cure.

Our annual deficits, the amount by which our federal expenses exceed our federal income each year, are the natural consequence of ignoring our national blueprint. In much the same way that attempting to add ten feet to an upstairs bedroom is not only financially prohibitive but also structurally unsound, so, too, are our federal deficits the logical and natural consequence of adding programs and responsibilities to the federal government that the blueprint and resultant structure were never designed to accommodate. The result has been not only the waste of billions of dollars, but also the creation of a national structure destined to collapse.

A GIFT-HOUSE CALAMITY

To fully understand our annual federal budget deficits, they must be considered in the context of overall federal spending. When I consider our annual deficits in this light, I am reminded of a fellow who several years ago inherited a very large and beautiful mansion in Atlanta, Georgia. He had inherited it from a distant relative and thought it to be a really incredible stroke of good fortune that he and his family would have the opportunity to move from the medium-size house in which they had been living to this gracious mansion.

Although the mansion had been given to him absolutely debt-free, after living in the home just a few months, he began to wonder whether his inheritance was such a stroke of good fortune after all. Since moving in, he had received his property tax bills, which alone were far more than the combined mortgage payments and taxes on his previous house. Next, he had found that the upkeep in terms of electricity, gas, maintenance of the grounds, painting, and insurance exceeded his ability to pay. Before long, he and his wife were both working second jobs trying to keep the mansion maintained.

As the bills continued to roll in, he and his wife began to meet regularly to try to find where they could make cuts in their personal budgets. After depleting their savings and working to the point of exhaustion, it occurred to them that they simply could not make enough money from their regular jobs to live there. Even with income from second jobs and in spite of all their budget cuts, they could not afford such a spacious, inefficient, and expensive mansion.

Finally, although both were reluctant to sell a mansion that had been in the family for so many years, they came to the conclusion that they simply could not afford not to sell it. In the final analysis, they sold it not only because they couldn't afford it financially, but also because they had come to realize that the stress and strain of keeping it up were destroying their marriage and their individual lives.

After reaching their decision, they put their mansion on the market, sold it, and moved back into the home in which they had once lived. Not surprisingly, they soon found that they really enjoyed their smaller home far more, because by living in a home they could afford and that was correctly designed for their needs, they had money available to do some of the things they really enjoyed doing. Today they are relieved and far happier than they were when they were slaves to their unaffordable mansion.

Their story reminds me of our own federal deficits because I think that if we really examine our deficit crisis today, we will find that it actually rests more in the fact that we have created a structure we cannot afford than it does in the idea that we haven't raised taxes enough or cut *essential* federal spending enough.

GROWTH OF THE BUDGET

A study of the growth in the federal budget over the past several decades vividly illustrates the point. Figure 4.1 sets forth the growth in federal revenues and outlays for each fiscal year from 1960 to 1987.

In 1960, the year John Kennedy was elected president, federal expenditures consumed 18.2 percent of our gross national product (GNP). Our GNP is simply another way of saying our national income. By 1980, the end of the Carter Administration, federal expenditures consumed 22.1 percent of GNP. In 1986, federal expenditures had grown to the point that they consumed almost 24 percent of GNP. For all intents and purposes, one-quarter of the American economic pie is now being consumed by federal expenditures. This fact is significant because the federal government is incapable of using these capital resources to create new wealth—it can only consume or redistribute the hard-earned wages and wealth of American workers.

Every dollar spent by the federal government is one less dollar available to individuals, families, churches, synagogues, city governments, county governments, state governments, or the private sector in general. Specifically, each dollar spent by the federal government is one dollar that is taken from our capital base

FIGURE 4.1
SUMMARY OF REVENUES, EXPENDITURES, AND THE NATIONAL DEBT

FISCAL YEAR	REVENUES			EXPENDITURES			SURPLUS OR DEFICITS (−)			NAT'L DEBT*
	Total $	1982 $	% of GNP	Total $	1982 $	% of GNP	Total $	1982 $	% of GNP	Total $
1960	92.5	341.6	18.3	92.2	340.1	18.2	0.3	1.1	0.1	290.9
1961	94.4	342.9	18.2	97.7	355.0	18.9	−3.3	−12.1	0.6	292.9
1962	99.7	358.4	17.9	106.8	384.1	19.2	−7.1	−25.7	1.3	303.3
1963	106.6	368.5	18.1	111.3	384.9	18.9	−4.7	−16.4	0.8	310.8
1964	112.6	383.0	17.9	118.5	403.2	18.8	−5.9	−20.1	0.9	316.8
1965	116.8	390.2	17.4	118.2	394.9	17.6	−1.4	−4.7	0.2	323.1
1966	130.8	419.6	17.7	134.5	431.5	18.2	−3.7	−11.9	0.5	329.5
1967	148.8	461.9	18.7	157.5	488.7	19.8	−8.6	−26.8	1.1	341.3
1968	153.0	451.5	18.0	178.1	525.8	21.0	−25.2	−74.3	3.0	369.8
1969	186.9	519.4	20.1	183.6	510.4	19.8	3.2	9.0	0.3	367.1
1970	192.8	502.0	19.5	195.6	509.4	19.8	−2.8	−7.4	0.3	382.6
1971	187.1	453.6	17.7	210.2	504.4	19.9	−23.0	−55.8	2.2	409.5
1972	207.3	474.2	18.0	230.7	527.6	20.0	−23.4	−53.5	2.0	437.3
1973	230.8	495.5	18.0	245.7	527.5	19.2	−14.9	−32.0	1.2	468.4
1974	263.2	516.6	18.6	269.4	528.7	19.0	−6.1	−12.0	0.4	486.2
1975	279.1	492.1	18.3	332.3	586.0	21.8	−53.2	−93.9	3.5	544.1
1976	298.1	488.9	17.6	371.8	609.8	21.9	−73.7	−120.9	4.3	631.9
1977	355.6	541.0	18.4	409.2	622.6	21.2	−53.6	−81.6	3.3	646.4
1978	399.6	568.0	18.4	458.7	652.2	21.1	−59.2	−84.1	2.7	780.4
1979	463.3	607.5	18.9	503.5	660.2	20.6	−40.2	−52.7	1.6	833.7
1980	517.1	611.7	19.4	590.9	699.1	22.1	−73.8	−87.3	2.8	914.3
1981	599.3	642.0	20.1	678.2	726.5	22.7	−78.9	−84.6	2.6	1,003.9
1982	617.8	617.8	19.7	745.7	745.7	23.8	−127.9	−128.0	4.1	1,147.0
1983	600.6	576.9	18.1	808.3	777.6	24.3	−207.7	−200.7	6.3	1,381.9
1984	666.5	618.1	18.1	851.8	789.9	23.1	−185.3	−171.9	5.0	1,576.8
1985	734.1	657.8	18.6	946.3	848.0	24.0	−212.3	−190.2	5.4	1,827.2
1986	769.1	673.0	18.5	989.8	866.2	23.8	−220.7	−193.2	5.3	2,132.9
1987 (est.)	834.1	708.2	19.0	1,019.9	865.9	23.6	−185.8	−157.7	4.3	2,372.4

SOURCE: *Historical Tables, Budget of the United States Government, fiscal year 1988.* Executive Office of the President, Office of Management and Budget. U.S. Government Printing Office: Washington, D.C., 1987. Tables 1.1; 1.2.

NOTE: All amounts in billions of dollars. Figures may not add to totals because of rounding.

*End of the year amount.

that could otherwise be used to create productive jobs, products for domestic and foreign consumption, and wealth from which basic private necessities and charity can be provided.

Prior to 1975, the federal government, except in times of war, never spent more than approximately 19 percent of GNP. Since that time, it has ever so gradually increased that percentage to the point that it is now literally stifling the private sector. If the federal government could finance its total operation during the first nineteen decades of our nation's existence for an annual total of approximately 19 percent of GNP, isn't it reasonable to believe that it can do so again?

Certainly it is, but this can only be achieved if the American people say no to those in Congress, or those who run for Congress, who continue to argue that the federal government can't survive on 19 percent of GNP. Today, a majority in the U.S. Congress are calling for a tax increase. In doing so, they are really saying that the federal government can't survive on that percentage of GNP. They're also saying that the budget of the federal government is more important than the budgets of American families and American businesses.

INCREASES IN ENTITLEMENT AND INTEREST PAYMENTS

Much of the reason for this growth in federal spending and the call for new taxes is the expansion of entitlements (payments to which individuals are automatically entitled because of previous laws passed by Congress) and the increase in interest payments on our national debt, which has accumulated as a result of years of the federal government's spending more than its annual revenues. Together, entitlement and interest payments represent 60 percent of the total federal budget (see figures 4.2 and 4.4). Payments to individuals now make up 45 percent of our budget. Interest on our debt makes up 15 percent of our budget. In 1986, interest payments averaged more than $350 million per day.

The growth in these two areas of the budget has not received the publicity that has been focused on the argument that the annual deficits under the Reagan Administration are the result of a combination of tax cuts and a growth in the defense budget.

In fact, the growth in entitlement and interest payments has far outpaced the growth in defense expenditures and tax cuts. Figures 4.2 and 4.3 speak for themselves with respect to how much we are now spending in constant dollars (that is, dollars adjusted for inflation) for entitlements and defense in compari-

FIGURE 4.2
EXPENDITURES FOR NATIONAL DEFENSE AND ENTITLEMENTS

FISCAL YEAR	NATIONAL DEFENSE				ENTITLEMENTS (PAYMENT TO INDIVIDUALS)			
	Total $	1982 $	% of Outlays	% of GNP	Total $	1982 $	% of Outlays	% of GNP
1960	48.1	192.1	52.2	9.5	24.2	73.2	26.2	4.8
1961	49.6	195.2	50.8	9.6	27.5	82.2	28.2	5.3
1962	52.3	202.2	49.0	9.4	28.9	85.2	27.1	5.2
1963	53.4	197.1	48.0	9.1	30.9	89.6	27.8	5.3
1964	54.8	198.8	46.2	8.7	32.2	91.6	27.2	5.1
1965	50.6	181.4	42.8	7.5	33.1	92.7	28.0	4.9
1966	58.1	197.9	43.2	7.9	37.0	101.3	27.5	5.0
1967	71.4	235.1	45.4	9.0	43.2	114.6	27.4	5.4
1968	81.9	254.8	46.0	9.6	49.8	128.0	27.9	5.9
1969	82.5	243.4	44.9	8.9	57.1	140.6	31.1	6.1
1970	81.7	225.6	41.8	8.3	64.7	152.2	33.1	6.5
1971	78.9	202.7	37.5	7.5	80.4	181.0	38.3	7.6
1972	79.2	190.9	34.3	6.9	92.9	200.1	40.3	8.1
1973	76.7	175.1	31.2	6.0	104.5	215.7	42.5	8.2
1974	79.3	163.3	29.5	5.6	120.1	228.3	44.6	8.5
1975	86.5	159.8	26.0	5.7	153.5	265.8	46.2	10.1
1976	89.6	153.6	24.1	5.3	180.1	291.7	48.4	10.6
1977	97.2	154.3	23.8	5.0	196.3	295.5	48.0	10.2
1978	104.5	155.0	22.8	4.8	211.0	296.8	46.0	9.7
1979	116.3	159.0	23.1	4.8	232.9	301.6	46.3	9.5
1980	134.0	164.0	22.7	5.0	277.5	324.7	47.0	10.4
1981	157.5	171.4	23.2	5.3	323.4	344.3	47.7	10.8
1982	185.3	185.3	24.9	5.9	356.7	356.7	47.8	11.4
1983	209.9	201.3	26.0	6.3	395.3	378.6	48.9	11.9
1984	227.4	211.5	26.7	6.2	399.8	368.7	46.9	10.8
1985	252.7	228.7	26.7	6.4	425.6	379.3	45.0	10.8
1986	273.4	242.1	27.6	6.6	448.0	389.4	45.3	10.8

SOURCE: *Historical Tables, Budget of the United States Government, fiscal year 1988.* Executive Office of the President, Office of Management and Budget. U.S. Government Printing Office: Washington, D.C., 1987. Tables 6.1; 6.2.

NOTE: All amounts in billions of dollars.

son to what we have historically spent in constant dollars in these two areas.

The figures conclusively show that today we're spending nearly 3 percentage points *less* on defense in terms of GNP and nearly 25 percent less as a percentage of our total federal budget than we were in 1960. Comparisons are made in constant dollars and as percentages of GNP or percentages of the total budget because inflation makes any direct comparison of 1960 dollars to 1986 dollars misleading. A direct, nonadjusted comparison would be the equivalent of saying that a person who in 1960 was paying $85 a month in rent for an average, three-bedroom apartment is now living far more extravagantly because he's paying $450 a month for the same three-bedroom flat.

If we're spending almost three percentage points less as a percentage of GNP on defense today than we were in 1960, why does it seem as though we're spending so much more on defense? The answer is that by the end of the Carter Administration, we had allowed our nation's defense system to deteriorate to the point that we were spending only 5 percent of GNP, almost half of what we spent in 1960. Fortunately, there has been an increase in defense spending under the Reagan Administration relative to what we were spending on defense at the end of the Carter Administration—a time, we should recall, when we couldn't even send our helicopters across the desert to rescue the hostages in Iran without half of them failing because of lack of maintenance and a lack of know-how on the part of our servicemen who operated them.

Relative to the last four decades, however, we are still spending substantially less on defense. During the past several years we have gradually built our defense system back up to the levels necessary for basic competence and protection. And as a percentage of GNP, to give you another point of comparison, we still spend substantially less on defense than we did in

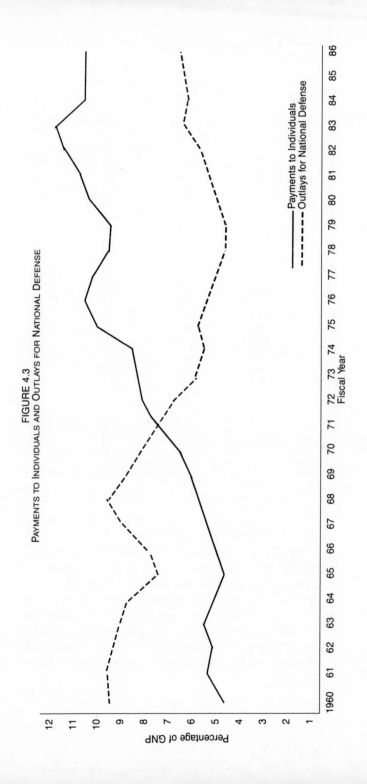

FIGURE 4.3
PAYMENTS TO INDIVIDUALS AND OUTLAYS FOR NATIONAL DEFENSE

——— Payments to Individuals
– – – – Outlays for National Defense

Percentage of GNP

Fiscal Year

FIGURE 4.4
EXPENDITURES FOR THE NET INTEREST PAYMENT
ON THE NATIONAL DEBT

Fiscal Year	Current $	Constant $	% of Total Outlay	% of Total GNP
1960	6.9	22.3	7.5	1.4
1961	6.7	21.4	6.9	1.3
1962	6.9	21.5	6.4	1.2
1963	7.7	23.8	7.0	1.3
1964	8.2	24.8	6.9	1.3
1965	8.6	25.4	7.3	1.3
1966	9.4	27.0	7.0	1.3
1967	10.3	28.6	6.5	1.3
1968	11.1	29.8	6.2	1.3
1969	12.7	32.4	6.9	1.4
1970	14.3	34.7	7.4	1.5
1971	14.8	34.0	7.1	1.4
1972	15.5	33.6	6.7	1.3
1973	17.3	35.9	7.1	1.4
1974	21.4	41.1	8.0	1.5
1975	23.2	40.4	7.0	1.5
1976	26.7	43.0	7.2	1.6
1977	29.9	44.6	7.3	1.5
1978	35.4	49.4	7.7	1.6
1979	42.6	54.7	8.5	1.7
1980	52.5	62.2	8.9	2.0
1981	68.7	73.6	10.1	2.3
1982	85.0	85.0	11.4	2.7
1983	89.8	86.3	11.1	2.7
1984	111.1	103.0	13.0	3.0
1985	129.4	115.5	13.7	3.3
1986	136.0	119.0	13.7	3.3
1987(est.)	143.6	121.9	14.0	3.3

SOURCE: *Historical Tables, Budget of the United States Government, fiscal year 1988*. Executive Office of the President, Office of Management and Budget. U.S. Government Printing Office: Washington, D.C., 1987. Tables 6.1; 6.2.

NOTE: All amounts in billions of dollars. Constant dollars are 1982 dollars.

1960, a peacetime period well after the Korean Conflict and before the Vietnam War.

While defense must accept its fair share of the belt-tightening necessary if we are to balance the federal budget, it must be remembered that too much of a cut in defense can, in the long run, be penny-wise and dollar-foolish. This is true because the federal government must always provide for an adequate defense system, and that defense system must be determined on the basis of the external threat, not simply our internal debt.

Certainly the world in future years is likely to continue becoming more dangerous rather than less dangerous. Accordingly, our defense needs will increase rather than decrease. By cutting unwisely today, we will have to pay even more in the future. It's actually far less expensive to maintain an adequate defense system than it is to let it deteriorate, as we did under the Carter Administration, and then try to build it back up. Because of the neglect during the late 1970s, it has been extremely expensive, but nonetheless necessary, to rebuild our defense system. It would be foolish to repeat the same mistake now simply because we refuse to cut nonessential federal spending.

One other point needs to be made about cuts in defense spending just for the sake of making cuts. Such cuts inevitably occur in two areas: salaries for our enlisted personnel, and contracts for existing weapons system. By cutting the salaries of our enlisted personnel, the sophisticated equipment we have purchased is rendered less effective, because that equipment is only as good as those who operate and monitor it.

As to cuts in existing contracts, such cuts can be extremely costly because the cuts occur at a point where production is most cost effective. Since research and development costs are built into the life of a contract, the first products off the assembly line are far more expensive than the last. The prototype of any weapons system is vastly more expensive than is the last unit produced. By terminating contracts, the research and development costs, which have already been paid, cannot be spread across the entire life of the contract.

To summarize, it is misleading to argue that our recent defense buildup is causing our annual deficits, because throughout the entirety of the Kennedy Administration we spent between 9 and 10 percent of GNP, and approximately *half* the total budget, on defense. Today we are spending between 6 and 7 percent of GNP and about 28 percent of the total budget on defense, *barely more than one-fourth*. It is thus evident that our budget deficits have not been caused by increases in the defense budget.

THE FEDERAL TAX TAKE

All that's necessary to counter the argument that our continuing annual deficits are the result of the tax cuts which have occurred under the Reagan Administration is to examine the amount of money the federal government now collects compared to what it has historically collected. Such an examination is important, because many are convinced that the federal deficits in recent years have resulted from the federal government's collecting less in taxes under the Reagan Administration than it did under the Carter Administration. This is simply not true. In 1987, individuals will pay more than $364 billion in federal income taxes, and corporations will pay more than $104 billion. That is $39.4 billion, or nearly 70 percent more in federal income taxes from corporations, and $120 billion, or 50 percent, more from individuals than were paid in 1980.

Much of the reason for this misperception is that politicians talk a lot about the tax cuts that were part of the Economic Recovery Act of 1981. Unfortunately, those same politicians don't talk about the tax increases that have followed, nor do they acknowledge the increase in revenues that has resulted from the economic expansion that has occurred since 1982.

In addition to income taxes, Americans pay substantial amounts in other federal taxes ranging from social security taxes to numerous excise taxes. In 1980, the total federal revenue collections were $517 billion. In 1987, they will be $842 billion. In constant dollars adjusted to take inflation into account, the federal government will collect $104 billion more in revenues in 1987 than it did in 1980.

What is truly amazing is that Congress has the audacity to consider a tax increase for fiscal year 1988, on the pretense of reducing the 1988 deficit, when revenues are already projected to increase significantly. Because of our continued economic expansion, revenues in 1988 will increase by more than $65 billion over revenues in 1987. Those in Congress who support new taxes are really saying a $65 billion increase is not enough; individual and family budgets must give way once again to an ever-expanding federal budget.

A FEDERAL
SPENDING SPREE

The fact of the matter is that we have a deficit today, not because the American people are taxed too little, but because the federal government is spending too much. Simple as it is, that point is the key to understanding our deficit. In fact, since the Reagan Administration's inception in 1981, federal revenues have increased by 41 percent (far more than the rate of inflation, which totaled 25 percent during the same period), but remarkably, spending has increased by more than 50 percent.

The growth of our federal budget and our government's practice of spending more than it collects in revenues is not a new phenomenon, but it is a phenomenon that has been increasing in intensity over the last several years. Figure 4.1 demonstrates the root of our problem and the gradual rate at which things have been getting worse. The trend is undeniable; both federal receipts and federal expenditures as a percentage of GNP have been gradually increasing since 1960. Although the trend of increasing the rate of federal spending has decreased slightly under the Reagan Administration, recent congressional actions indicate that the trend will continue at an even greater rate in the future. In short, we have experienced annual deficits because the rate of growth in spending has been outpacing the rate of growth in receipts.

In addition to the various federal taxes, which in the aggregate represent over 19 percent of GNP, average state and local taxes now total another 10 percent of GNP. In other words, federal, state, and local taxes now claim nearly one-third of our national income. That is 8 percent more of GNP than was the case in 1950, when total federal tax receipts were 14.8 percent of GNP and total state and local taxes were 6.2 percent.

In 1950, looking at it from the other side, 80 percent of our national income remained in the private sector, where it could be reinvested to create new jobs, to manufacture products for export or domestic consumption, and to be spent by individuals, families, churches, synagogues, and private organizations. Today, however, only 71 percent is available for these same purposes. And even more sobering, the trend of ever greater government confiscation of private wealth and earnings is ominously clear.

THE CULPRIT:
TRANSFER PAYMENTS

The increase in federal social spending in general, and direct payments to individuals in particular, is the reason for our deficits. As can be clearly seen by examining Figures 4.2 and 4.3, from 1960 to 1980, direct payments to individuals increased in direct proportion to the degree that defense spending decreased. In 1960, direct payments to individuals comprised roughly 26 percent of the total budget, or 4.8 percent of GNP. In 1980, the last year of the Carter Administration, direct payments to individuals comprised roughly 47 percent of the total budget, or 10.4 percent of GNP.

What we have actually done over the course of the last quarter of a century is to reverse our priorities. Rather than spending half the entire budget on defense and one-fourth on direct payments to individuals, defense now makes up roughly one-quarter of the budget, while roughly half is now spent on direct payments to individuals. As we have doubled transfer entitlement payments to individuals, we have reduced by 50 percent the amount we spend on defense as a percentage of the total federal budget.

The trend of increased payments to individuals and decreased defense spending is extremely significant from a constitutional perspective, because the Constitution places the responsibility of providing for our national defense exclusively on the federal government. There is no similar provision in the Constitution respecting the economic redistribution of the nation's wealth.

CONGRESS CAN'T BE TRUSTED WITH ANY TAX INCREASE

Even if we were to raise taxes again, there is absolutely no reason to believe that Congress would use the additional revenue to reduce the annual deficits or to repay our accumulated debt. In fact, recent history demonstrates that exactly the opposite would occur. As recently as 1982, President Reagan reluctantly agreed with Congress to raise taxes as a means of reducing the deficit. To obtain the president's approval of the tax increase contained in the Tax Equity and Fiscal Responsibility Act of 1982 (TEFRA) legislation that he signed, the Congress promised to reduce spending by three dollars for every dollar raised by the new taxes.

TEFRA became law, and so did the new taxes. Predictably, however, Congress not only failed to satisfy its promise to cut spending, it actually matched every new dollar raised by the new tax with a $1.14 increase in new spending! In fact, a recent study conducted for Congress's Joint Economic Committee reveals that from 1947 to 1986, every time Congress raised taxes by one dollar, federal spending increased by an average of $1.58. To again raise taxes on the premise of reducing the deficit is like hoping to put out a raging fire by pouring gasoline on it, or like giving a drug addict money in hopes that he will pay his debts.

"Cuts"—Washington Style

If, as a result of the current economic recovery, TEFRA, and other legislation that has raised taxes, we

FIGURE 4.5
COMPOSITION OF FEDERAL EXPENDITURES

Category	1980	1981	1982	1983	1984	1985	1986	1987 (ests.)
National Defense	134.0	157.5	185.3	209.9	227.4	252.7	273.4	279.6
Social Security	118.5	139.5	156.0	170.7	178.2	188.6	198.8	207.9
Interest on the Debt	52.5	68.7	85.0	89.8	111.1	129.4	136.0	143.6
Income Security	86.5	99.7	107.7	123.7	112.7	128.2	119.8	124.2
Medicare	32.1	39.2	46.6	52.6	57.5	65.8	70.2	73.7
Health	23.2	26.9	27.5	28.6	30.4	33.5	35.9	40.3
Agriculture	8.8	11.3	15.9	22.9	13.6	25.6	31.5	30.2
Veteran Benefits and Services	21.2	23.0	24.0	24.8	25.6	26.3	26.4	26.2
Transportation	21.3	23.4	20.6	21.3	23.7	25.8	28.1	25.4
Education Elementary, Secondary, Vocational, Higher	13.6	16.0	14.0	13.5	13.9	15.8	16.3	15.4
International Affairs	12.7	13.1	12.3	11.9	15.9	16.2	14.2	13.8
Other	66.6	59.9	50.8	39.8	41.8	38.5	39.3	39.6
Total	590.9	678.2	745.7	808.3	851.8	946.3	989.8	1,019.9

SOURCE: *Historical Tables, Budget of the United States Government, fiscal year 1988.* Executive Office of the President, Office of Management and Budget. U.S. Government Printing Office: Washington, D.C., 1987. Table 3.3

NOTE: All amounts in billions of dollars.

have increased federal revenues by 41 percent during the past five years and we are regularly told by politicians that Congress has been cutting federal spending, how is it possible that today we have annual deficits that are even larger than they were in 1981?

The answer is that we have *not* been cutting expenditures—unless you define "cuts" as those in Congress define cuts. In Congress, a cut is defined as spending less money next year than you wanted to spend, but more money than you spent last year. You can go through the federal budget, line item after line item, and you'll find the same thing: since 1981, federal programs and expenditures have *increased* rather than decreased. Figure 4.5 reveals that virtually every category of the budget has increased rather than decreased since 1981.

Overall federal spending in 1981 was $678.2 billion, compared to 1987 federal spending that will top $1 trillion, an increase of over $300 billion. When accounting for inflation, federal spending still increased by nearly $140 billion during the same period. Despite these facts, however, the American people have been told by the media and by many from Congress that there have been severe cuts in expenditures under the Reagan Administration.

LIVING IN AN UNAFFORDABLE STRUCTURE

Statistics can be overwhelming, and trying to sort them all out can be difficult at best, but one fundamental truth can be derived from our federal budget statistics. Today our nation is living in a budget structure that it simply cannot afford. Faced with this incontrovertible fact, our nation can continue its futile attempts to shave spending here and there by making marginal savings in either this program or that program, or it can recognize that, just as the family in my illustration was incapable of continuing to live in the mansion they inherited, so, too, are we as a nation incapable of continuing to live within the structural budget we have inherited from current and past Congresses. The time has now come for us to structurally change our federal budget so that it conforms to the foundation called for in the Constitution, our original blueprint.

The only other alternative is to throw away the original blueprint and design a new one with an entirely different foundation. If we are to choose such an alternative, however, it ought to be only after much debate and deliberation, and there should be a constitutional amendment reflecting such a deliberate decision.

Consequences Are More than Financial

The consequences of ignoring the division of responsibilities set forth in our Constitution have been more than financial. The results have been equally profound in those areas where the federal government has exceeded its constitutional authority and encroached on responsibilities of parents and state and local governments. In subsequent chapters we will examine the effects such encroachments have had on educational policy, welfare dependency, and First Amendment rights.

A CONSTITUTIONAL SOLUTION

When the adverse consequences of ignoring our Constitution are considered clearly and rationally, it becomes increasingly apparent that the only wise choice for us is to reembrace the constitutional blueprint that has served us so well in the past. The most effective way to achieve this objective is by adopting a constitutional amendment that requires a balanced federal budget and, at the same time, limits annual federal expenditures to a fixed percentage of GNP. A logical figure would be 19 percent, because such an amount would avoid the necessity of raising taxes. It also recognizes that with the exception of times of war and national emergencies—that is, as a general rule—we operated efficiently and effectively for more than 175 years at an amount equal to or less than 19 percent of GNP.

Because the only exception to this general rule has been during times of war or national emergencies, such a constitutional amendment should recognize and provide for such exceptions. To declare a national emergency should require a two-thirds vote of both the House and Senate, just as is presently required for Congress to declare war.

To allow our national economy to adjust gradually to this decrease in federal expenditures, the reductions should be phased in over a period of five years. In year one, federal expenditures should be reduced by 1 percent of GNP, from 24 percent to 23; in year two, from 23 percent to 22; and so on until year five, when the 19 percent figure would be achieved and subsequently maintained. A balanced budget is desirable, but it shouldn't be achieved too quickly for much the same reason that a drug addict ought to be gradually withdrawn from a drug dependency. Just as a "cold turkey" withdrawal can kill a severely addicted person, so, too, could a "cold turkey" withdrawal from addictive federal spending adversely affect our national economy.

Such an amendment would not only lead to an elimination of deficit spending, but in the process Congress would also be forced to prioritize its spending, just as every American is now required to do. Most significantly, federal control and power would shrink in proportion to its decreased revenues and expenditures.

FAMILY BUDGET PROCESS—CONGRESS TAKE NOTE

In establishing budget priorities, now and after the ratification of a balanced budget amendment, Congress could certainly learn a great deal by examining the average American family's budget process. In approaching its own budget, the average family sits down and asks itself, "How much do we reasonably expect to earn next year?" Then, based on that expectation of earnings, the family asks itself, "How do we want to spend that money?"

Now, the family certainly doesn't start by assuming it's going to earn the same thing that some other family, say the family next door, is expecting to earn. Instead the family asks, "What do we *reasonably* expect to earn?" They don't start by asking, "What would we *like* to earn?" Rational individuals recognize that the logical starting point is what they have earned in the past several years.

After answering these basic questions, the average family sits down and determines how it is going to spend its anticipated income. The starting point is to determine how much must be spent for necessities such as food, clothing, and shelter. Next the family allocates an amount for transportation costs necessary to get to and from work and to get to and from play and all its other activities. Finally, after taking care of all the essentials, the family asks, "With respect to what's left, what are our priorities?"

Most families are going to have a wide divergence of opinions about what their spending priorities ought to be. Chances are the teenagers are going to say they want a new stereo. The father is going to say he would like a new set of golf clubs. The mother is going to say that she would rather see Dad get a new lawn mower.

After all the various special interests within the family are considered, at some point there must be a recognition that there's a limited amount of money available and some tough choices must be made. Decisions must be made between whether to buy a new stereo or a new lawn mower. Once those choices are made, a budget emerges based on those choices. Of course, the budget is of value only if it is followed.

The Budget-Busting Calamity

What happens if the family ignores its budget? At some point it will find that if it has spent more in a given area than it budgeted, there's now insufficient money to buy something essential, like food. If the family is to continue to eat, it's now necessary, assuming the family is credit-worthy, to go out and borrow the money necessary to feed the family.

If a family ignores its budget year after year, however, whoever is lending the money to cover its deficit-spending habits is going to say at some point, "Wait a minute. I can't continue to lend your family additional money when all you're doing is paying me interest and at the same time adding to the principal amount of your debt. Before I can lend you any additional money, you're going to have to show me some fundamental change in the way your family is formulating and following its budget. Otherwise I'm not only doing a disservice to myself, but I'm also doing a disservice to you and your family."

In other words, any lender is going to say, "You've got to understand that you're living above your means, and if you don't stop living that way, you and your family are going to find yourselves in a state of bankruptcy."

It was Alexander Hamilton, one of the chief architects of our nation's financial system, who said, "In framing a government which is to be administered by men over men the great difficulty lies in this: You must first enable the government to control the governed, and in the next place, oblige it to control itself."[1] Hamilton must have had some kind of premonition about the difficulty the American government would have in later years exercising control over its own compulsive spending habits.

THE FEDERAL GOVERNMENT IS NO DIFFERENT

The Congress of the United States and the federal government are no different from the average American family in the sense that they are bound by the same laws of economics. Prolonged deficit spending inevitably leads to national bankruptcy. There are no exceptions to this fundamental law of economics.

If a family knew that it didn't have to make tough choices between the conflicting interests of various family members, it is doubtful that the family would ever make such choices voluntarily. Without limitations on how much it's allowed to borrow and spend, Congress will likewise never voluntarily make difficult choices.

When it comes to making tough choices, Congress reminds me of the time I took my two-and-a-half-year-old daughter Kelley shopping for toys. After spending less than five minutes in the toy department, Kelley had selected three toys she wanted me to buy for her. I told her she would have to choose her favorite, because I would buy only one. She responded by telling me they were all her favorites and she wanted me to buy them all. She simply could not decide between them.

Just as I was about to give in to Kelley, her mom stepped in and with her most stern voice told us both that we could afford only one. If Kelley couldn't choose just one, she wouldn't get any. Within seconds, Kelley had made her choice.

In a very real sense, Congress has never been forced to make tough choices. When confronted with difficult decisions, it has simply avoided making them by borrowing the money, thereby adding to the national debt; by printing more money, thereby reducing the purchasing power of the American people; by increasing taxes, thereby telling families to cut *their* budgets; or by exercising a combination of all three of these alternatives. All are cop-outs, and all have had adverse effects on the American economy and every American family.

When Congress borrows the money to finance its spending sprees, it places an unnecessary demand on our national savings, which would otherwise be available for lending to individuals and businesses who need capital to buy homes, start new businesses, or expand existing ones. The result is almost always an increase in interest rates. When interest rates rise, many can't afford to start new businesses or expand existing ones. This in turn reduces the number of new jobs that would otherwise be created, and a rise in unemployment rates follows. Another effect of increased interest rates is that the purchase of a new or first home becomes more difficult or even impossible. This in turn adversely affects those employed in the housing industry.

If the government prints more money, it reduces the value of the money Americans have worked so hard to earn. The net result of printing additional money is inflation, and inflation hurts most those who are on fixed and low incomes, the poor and the aged. Increased inflation has much the same adverse impact on new businesses and the ability of individuals to buy a home that increased interest rates have. Similarly, as businesses are affected, so, too, are the number of new jobs and unemployment rates.

When it raises taxes, Congress takes money away from families and businesses and, in effect, causes the same impact as increased interest rates and inflation. By raising taxes, Congress is actually saying it is better capable of spending your money than you are.

RESTORING THE RESTRAINTS ON GOVERNMENT

The blueprint set forth in the Constitution calls for a federal government of limited size, scope, and costs, not only because the Framers understood the need to place fiscal restraints on the Congress, but also because they knew our society as a whole would function better. Most Americans oppose increases in taxes as well as the resulting increases in the size and costs of the federal government because they know we can't afford to allow the federal government to continue growing without restraint, and also because in the past the results of uncontrolled growth have been disastrous. In direct proportion to the degree that the size and responsibilities of the federal government have increased, the welfare rolls have expanded, the quality of education has declined, and the federal government's administration of justice has faltered.

Thus, the strongest argument for restraining the federal government in accordance with the provisions of the Constitution is not the argument that we can't afford the growth of the federal government financially, but that we can't afford it in terms of what it's doing to our moral and economic fiber. Had the growth of the federal government resulted in the *reduction* of welfare dependency and net poverty, an *improved* quality of public education, and a *consistent* administration of justice, a strong case could be made for finding a way to finance the growth and even accommodating future growth. The reality, however, is that past growth has failed to achieve the results that have been relentlessly promised as each expansion has been sought and achieved.

Federal Squeeze on the Family

In addition, with the expansion of the federal government's responsibility into areas intended by the

Constitution to be assumed by the private sector, families, churches, and synagogues, these institutions have gradually been squeezed out. Nowhere is this more evident than in the breakdown of the American family, which has traditionally been the backbone of our nation. As the federal government has grown and its budget has expanded to finance that growth, the budgets of American families and businesses have had to be severely cut back.

Until measures are taken to force Congress to make tough budget choices, it will continue to raise taxes and print and borrow more money. Any of these methods of dealing with the problem, or any combination of these methods, ultimately hurts our national economy and the budgets of American families and businesses. Continued growth in federal expenditures will not only contribute to the continued demise of the American family, but to the continued demise of the American public education system, the individual and general welfare of all Americans, and the loss of our individual liberties as well.

WASHINGTON'S WARNING

It was George Washington who said, "Government is not reason, it is not eloquence—it is force! Like fire it is a dangerous servant and a fearful master; never for a moment should it be left to irresponsible action."[2] It was out of this respect for the fearsome power of unrestrained government that Washington and his colleagues sought to bind, check, and restrain the power of the central government. Their experience with King George had taught them the dangers of a runaway central government.

We have lost this healthy fear of a large, intrusive government, and year by year, bit by bit, we've been unleashing the fearsome monster our Founders fought to tether, all with the notion that it will only do us good. The Founders, on the other hand, knew well that the power to tax is the power to destroy.

We can bring the federal budget monster under control, we can reinstitute the fetters the Founders placed on the federal government, but only if we diagnose the real problem and take the cure quickly and decisively. The cure is a major operation, an operation that will cut back the federal government to the size our Founders knew was just right to keep our nation as a whole healthy, strong, and growing. The necessary operation is a constitutional amendment requiring a balanced federal budget at a level not to exceed a fixed percentage of our national income, preferably 19 percent of GNP. Such an operation will, of course, cause some pain. But the pain is preferable by far to the alternative.

TWO FIRST STEPS

Pending such an operation, there are a couple of measures that can be implemented to partially alleviate the problem.

A Line-Item Veto

The first is a line-item veto that would allow the president to veto any portion of an appropriation bill deemed to be excessive or unjustified. Under current law, the president must either accept an appropriation bill in its entirety or veto it in its entirety. The problem with such an approach is twofold. First, it forces the president to throw the baby out with the bathwater. By having to veto essential spending if he's to veto nonessential and wasteful spending, the president's real options are drastically limited and the veto mechanism written into the Constitution to allow the president to hold a fiscally irresponsible Congress in check is rendered virtually meaningless.

Second, because Congress now habitually combines numerous appropriations bills into "omnibus" spending bills, there is no effective way for the president to veto wasteful or nonessential items without totally shutting down the government. A veto of an omnibus spending bill can often terminate or dangerously hinder certain federal functions by terminating salaries for military and law enforcement personnel.

In fact, Congress ended the second session of the ninety-ninth Congress by passing one single omnibus spending bill that included *all* discretionary spending bills in one single package. The bill appropriated over $500 billion dollars, the largest single spending bill in the history of the world. Certainly our Founders never anticipated such an irresponsible and anonymous approach to governing. Armed only with the general veto power given him by the Constitution, the president was given a choice to sign the bill into law or shut the government down. The president understandably chose to sign the bill. The wisdom of his decision is subject to debate, but one thing is certain: had the president had a line-item veto, he would have used it and the American people would have been spared billions of dollars in unnecessary spending, taxing, and borrowing.

One of the most attractive aspects of a line-item veto would be the accountability that it would bring back to the congressional appropriation process. Under the current process, there is little accountability with respect to individual members of the House and Senate. Most members of Congress blame the Congress as an institution for deficit spending or, worse yet, the president.

The absurdity of blaming the president is that under the provisions of our Constitution, the president cannot appropriate any money whatsoever. Only Congress can appropriate money. Obviously, then, only Congress can be held accountable for our past and present deficit-spending practices.

A line-item veto would allow the American people to hold individual members of Congress, as well as Congress as an institution, accountable for how taxpayers' money is spent. By forcing members to vote for or against specific spending measures, individual members could no longer duck the accountability issue by saying they weren't voting for the wasteful portions of a particular bill, only for another portion.

Many have argued that a line-item veto is unconstitutional. Such an argument is both illogical and contradictory to the current veto power contained in the Constitution. How can it be unconstitutional to give the president power to do specifically what the president already has power to do generally? Speaking metaphorically, how can it be unconstitutional to give the president power to do with a scalpel what the president already has power to do with a machete? The intent of the Founders in giving the president a general veto power was to place a check on uncontrolled congressional spending. A line-item veto would achieve precisely that result.

Constitutional Justification

One other partial remedy to uncontrolled federal spending would be to require Congress to state with specificity in any proposed bill the constitutional justification for spending money authorized or appropriated by the bill. Such a requirement would at least force members of Congress to consider the clear language and intent of our Constitution.

REMEDIES—PARTIAL AND COMPLETE

While these two symptomatic remedies can be helpful in controlling our real problem, they can not be fully remedial. Just as my doctor's recommendation that I watch my diet and drink plenty of milk could not cure the real problem causing my stomach ulcers, neither can any measure short of an actual operation bring current congressional spending under total and permanent control. The operation is, as previously stated, a constitutional amendment requiring a balanced budget and limiting federal expenditures.

Because the stakes are so high, we must begin now to prepare for such an operation. Once performed, the operation will yield a permanent remedy to the problem of uncontrolled federal spending. Until the Constitution is amended to restore the original limitations on the size, scope, and costs of our federal government, we are in constant jeopardy of hemorrhaging. The sooner we can get to the operating room, the better.

5

Symptom: Mediocrity in Public Education

*I*n 1985, the following article in *USA Today,* with the headline "Parents Facing Hearing on 'Stealing' Education," caught my attention:

> The children are known as line jumpers; they live in one school district, but go to school in another.
>
> Prosecutors say their parents are each guilty of stealing $4,001 worth of education from Bloomfield, Conn.
>
> Four Hartford-area parents face a pre-trial hearing Wednesday on larceny charges. It's the first time in Connecticut and possibly in the USA that parents have been arrested and charged with stealing education in a residency dispute.
>
> "It's scary. I've never been to jail before," says Saundra Foster, one of the parents. If convicted, each faces up to 20 years in prison and a $10,000 fine.
>
> "It's worth going to jail," says Foster, a 34-year-old insurance company administrator. "My son should be able to go where he could get the best education."

The third-degree larceny charges brought against Mrs. Foster and three other parents were later dropped by the court, but the circumstances portrayed in this tragic story explain in part why I agreed to introduce a major education reform bill in the Ninety-ninth Congress. The bill, written by the Reagan Administration and entitled the Equity and Choice Act of 1985, commonly referred to as TEACH, was designed to radically change the role of the federal government in primary and secondary education. Based as a trial project on one specific federal program, the bill, if enacted, would have allowed—for the first time—*the parents* of educationally disadvantaged children to choose which elementary or high school would provide their children's education under the compensatory education program originally begun in 1965 as part of President Lyndon Johnson's Great Society.

TEACH provides for vouchers, not money, to be directed to parents of children eligible for Chapter 1 benefits. Instead of allowing educational authorities to take federal funds designated for the educationally disadvantaged to spend as they see fit, vouchers would be distributed directly to the parents, who could then redeem them for the educational services they determined could best benefit their child. The amount of these vouchers represent the money ($600 per child) already allowed in the program. Parents could use these vouchers to send their child to a public or private school in the same school district, or to a public or private school in another district. Mothers like Saundra Foster would greatly benefit from the freedom of choice and increased opportunity for direct involvement in the educational decisions regarding their children. In the same way, schools would benefit from the creation of healthy competition, important to achieve high standards in these programs.

SOCIALIZED EDUCATION

At the press conference when Secretary of Education William Bennett, Utah Senator Orrin Hatch, and I announced the introduction of the TEACH bill in the House and Senate, I stated that Americans have traditionally rejected the concept of socialized medicine because they prefer the quality and choice offered by the free enterprise system, compared to the mediocrity and limited selection of a government-run monopoly. Americans like to have the ability to pick and choose among the various medical providers, whether they be hospitals or physicians.

Another reason Americans have rejected socialized medicine is their disdain for dealing with bureaucrats and the inordinate amount of paperwork that inevitably characterizes any system of socialized service. History shows that in any socialized service system, an individual's ability to affect policy making is diminished in direct proportion to the size and monopolization of the bureaucracy. The net effect of socialized, government-controlled monopolies is mediocrity, inefficiency, and lack of meaningful choice.

In contrast, a private, free enterprise system is characterized by a direct relationship between the provider and patient. If a patient is dissatisfied with a provider's service, the patient can select a different provider or negotiate a reduction in payment to reflect his or her dissatisfaction. Similarly, a provider is free to provide or decline service to whomever the provider so chooses and to charge a rate that rewards excellence in product, management, and the services provided. A free enterprise system is neither stagnant nor unresponsive to specific interests and needs. In the final analysis, the net effect of a free enterprise system is improved quality, efficiency, and choice.

After contrasting the type of medical care provided in a socialized system to that provided in a free enterprise system, I concluded by stating that the American people have embraced, without ever deliberately

choosing to do so, the concept of socialized education. And as with the medical services, the net result
has been mediocrity, inefficiency, and lack of meaningful choice. As I made that statement, I saw that a
number in the national press corps were surprised at
my choice of words. In fact, after the press conference, one of the reporters telephoned to ask me if I
really intended to use the word *socialized* in describ-
ing our current primary and secondary public education system.

In response I said, "Sure I did, and let me explain
why. Let's compare the characteristics of socialized
medicine with the characteristics of our public education system as we find it in America today, at least inso-
far as it relates to the majority of public elementary
and high schools." I then summarized those characteristics.

The Lack of Choice

Certainly most public elementary and high schools
fail to provide parents with meaningful choice. That
lack of choice is exacerbated among those parents
who are least able to pay out of their own pocket for
their children's education. Specifically, the only
meaningful choice available to parents, with respect
to which public school their children attend, exists in
the context of being able to choose the neighborhood
in which they buy or rent a home. Thus, one of the
questions most parents ask when purchasing a home
is, "What about the public schools my children will
attend if we buy this home?"

Naturally parents take into consideration the quality of a neighborhood's public schools when buying a
house. If they don't like a particular school system,
they will most likely exercise their limited choice by
selecting a house in a neighborhood located in another school district more to their liking.

Regrettably, individuals who have meager incomes
are unable to exercise even this fairly limited avenue of
choice. Individuals with extremely limited economic

resources are assigned to a particular housing project, which in turn relegates them to a particular public school system. Even if low-income individuals are not assigned to a specific housing project, their choices, because of economic restraints, are very limited.

Because the quality of any school in the public system is necessarily dictated in large part by the politics of economics and affluence, those individuals who live in lower-income neighborhoods will attend, more often than not, a public school that is of relatively lower quality.

The truth of the matter is that by inadvertently allowing public education to become a socialized system, exempt from the pressures and restraints of a free enterprise system, we have compromised quality and improvement and have settled for a mediocrity that threatens the educational opportunities our children deserve and ultimately threatens our nation's future. If we are to reverse this dangerous trend, Americans must answer two fundamental questions: Is our objective to achieve the highest quality education financed at public expense? Or is our objective to perpetuate and protect our current public education system, even if that system denies parents authority and choice in the educational decisions affecting their children and, for the most part, is incapable of delivering the highest quality of education? We must choose between these two objectives, because our own recent history indicates that they are, in all likelihood, mutually exclusive.

To those who argue that our current system of elementary and high schools is the only way to provide quality public education, I would counter by saying that a superior system *is* possible, a system where, though financed by the public, it is not necessary for parents to yield responsibility for educating their children. An example of how this could work is found by examining our highly successful system for higher education. Today, parents and students have almost unrestrained options with respect to colleges they attend, whether public or private. The only real restraints in any student's choice are financial and intellectual ones, and these restraints will exist in any education system, be it public, private, or quasi-public. But even in these areas parents have a wide range of options from which to match financial capabilities and educational goals—from junior colleges and technical trade schools to the most prestigious public and private four-year institutions. At the college level, parents and students are not denied choice and varied opportunities.

Private colleges have for years been attended by students who receive federal funds. Veterans who attended public colleges and universities under the G.I. Bill made their own choices of the institutions of higher learning they attended. Convenience of location, areas of study, tuition expenses, and other factors all play roles in determining a student's selection—but the choices are varied and, most of all, available. Today the same is true for students attending public colleges using federal Pell grants. The grants are not applicable to just one neighboring public institution, but rather are applicable to any college or university that has accepted the applicant. The truth of the matter is, regarding elementary and secondary education, we are not allowing ourselves to think progressively enough to see beyond the restraints of our present system to the obvious benefits of a system based on free-enterprise competition and choice. Today, the national average for combined federal, state, and local expenditures on education for each child is nearly $4,200 per year. Imagine what options would be available to parents, rich or poor, white or black, if they could spend that same $4,200 per year on the school of their own choice.

The Lack of Competition

The same free-enterprise pressures that have contributed to the quality and independence of higher education in America can also improve quality if applied to primary and secondary education. At the same time, competitive pressures can return key educational decisions to parents and local school boards. Consider, for example, the following contrast between our higher education system and our primary and secondary education system.

Unlike our colleges and universities, public elementary and high schools have no meaningful competition. If parents wish to take advantage of federal, state, and local taxes they pay, they have no option but to send their children to the government-run schools to which they are assigned. The public school system is, in essence, a monopoly. If parents are dissatisfied with the quality of public education available, or with the performance of a particular public school, they have little if any direct way of expressing their dissatisfaction. Even if they get involved with the PTA or the politics of a local school board they will soon learn that many of the school's programs and policies are mandated from Washington.

As parents realize they are in a large part unable to affect policy, they eventually give up and either accept their plight with great frustration or, if they are able to do so, send their children to private schools or move to another neighborhood. Neither of the latter are options, however, if, like Saundra Foster, you can't afford to pay the costs of sending your children to a private school or of moving to another neighborhood.

The monopolistic system that now exists not only negatively affects the quality of education, but it also penalizes good teachers while rewarding mediocre ones. In many states, the national teachers' union, known as the National Education Association (NEA) has successfully defeated any attempts to establish a merit pay system wherein teachers are paid based on ability rather than length of tenure. Why are we surprised, then, when quality teachers eventually leave the system for higher paying and more satisfying careers? A system that fails to reward excellence and penalize mediocrity will inevitably lose many of its best teachers. There are, of course, those who will continue to teach in spite of these conditions because of their love of teaching and desire to see students learn. But why should these exceptional teachers go unrewarded by our system?

PUBLIC SCHOOLS NO LONGER MELTING POTS

One of the arguments frequently made in support of our current system is that it serves as a melting pot for students of varied racial, geographic, ethnic, academic, and economic backgrounds to learn together. These differences contribute to the overall educational experience.

While this was once a valid argument, it is becoming increasingly invalid. Because of the eroding quality of public education, increasing numbers of parents who can afford to do so are taking their children out of the public system. Those that lack the financial means to take their children out are left behind.

According to a front page article in the July 26, 1987, *New York Times,* researchers at the University of Chicago recently concluded that "the level of segregation of black students remained virtually unchanged between 1972 and 1984, with nearly two-thirds of blacks attending predominately minority schools." In light of the persistent segregation of minority students, the authors warned against the "deepening isolation of children growing up in inner-city ghettos and barrios from any contact with mainstream American society."

The reason for this disturbing trend is that segregation is now primarily a function of social and economic status. If we are serious about offering real educational opportunities to all Americans, we must attack the heart of the problem. Our current education system is perpetuating, rather than decreasing, the segregation and polarization of those who are in the lower social and economic classes. A free-enterprise school system, financed by the public sector, can reverse this undesirable and unnecessary trend.

MORE MONEY, LESS EDUCATION

Too Many Chiefs?

The continued federal influence and control of our public education systems over the past twenty-five years has been accompanied by a predictable increase in the number of administrators employed by the system. This increase has been vastly disproportionate to the growth in the number of pupils. In fact, during the period of time that the number of administrators was increasing significantly, the student enrollment was decreasing.

For example, in 1963 the number of administrators in all the public school systems in America was 92,201. At that time the total student enrollment was 40,187,000. By 1985, the number of administrators had more than doubled to 191,660. Yet during this period there was actually a decline in the number of students enrolled in our public schools. By 1985, student enrollment had fallen to 39,513,000.

Such a bureaucratic phenomenon is typical of any socialized system. In a socialized, government-run monopoly, the size of the bureaucracy grows in direct proportion to the amount of money appropriated.

There's also a point in such a system at which the larger the system becomes and the more it costs, the lesser the quality of the resulting product. This is exactly what has happened in the primary and secondary public education system in America. As you can see from Figure 5.1, during the same time period that the number of administrators doubled, per-student expenditures increased at a rate well in excess of inflation. The number of teachers and the amount of the average teacher's salary, however, remained relatively constant. Significantly, the student-teacher ratio improved primarily as a result of the decrease in the student population. The *only* explanation for the huge increase in per-student expenditures is that it was used to finance the growth and perpetuation of the bureaucracy.

Spending More, Getting Less

During this same time frame, quality dropped in direct proportion to the increase in the federal expenditures and growth of bureaucratic presence and control. In 1963, we were spending less than $1 billion at the federal level on all primary and secondary education programs. When that figure is adjusted for inflation, it translates to $3.2 billion in 1985–1986 constant dollars. At that time, the average total SAT score was 980, 478 on the verbal portion and 502 on the math portion. During the twenty-year period preceding 1963, average SAT scores had remained constant or had gradually increased. In 1963, the average combined federal, state, and local funds expended per pupil was $559 ($1,971 in 1985–1986 constant dollars).

In 1982, the average per-pupil combined expenditures had risen to $3,230 ($3,580 in 1985–1986 constant dollars), and the average total SAT score had declined to 893, 425 on the verbal portion and 468 on the math portion. Nor was 1982 an aberration; average SAT scores in America had been in a steady descent for nineteen straight years.

In 1981, the year average SAT scores bottomed out, we were spending a total of $8.2 billion ($9.5 billion in 1985–1986 constant dollars) on education at the federal level, three times as much money as was being spent on education at the federal level in 1963, the year average SAT scores peaked. When combined with state and local funding for education, the total average per student expenditure for education was

FIGURE 5.1

SAT SCORES AND EXPENDITURES FOR PUBLIC ELEMENTARY
AND SECONDARY SCHOOLS

School Year	Fall Enrollment K–12 (in millions)[a]	Average Teacher Salary[b]	School District Admin.[c]	Pupil/ Teacher Ratio[d]	Pupil/ Admin. Ratio[e]	Total Expend./ Student[f]	Federal Expend./ Student[g]	SAT Average[h]
1959–60	35,182	18,499	82,301	26.0	427.5	1,748	74.29	975
1960–61	—	—	—	—	—	—	—	—
1961–62	37,464	19,958	86,122	25.6	435.0	1,918	79.40	971
1962–63	—	—	—	—	—	—	—	—
1963–64	40,187	21,140	92,201	25.5	435.9	1,971	84.56	973
1964–65	—	—	—	—	—	—	—	—
1965–66	42,173	22,099	99,795	24.7	422.6	2,229	173.79	967
1966–67	—	—	—	—	—	—	—	—
1967–68	43,891	23,744	109,875	23.7	399.5	2,514	219.88	958
1968–69	—	—	—	—	—	—	—	—
1969–70	45,619	24,878	117,225	22.7	389.2	2,751	221.21	948
1970–71	45,909	25,396	—	22.3	—	2,874	242.40	943
1971–72	46,081	25,665	128,845	22.3	357.6	2,983	279.63	937
1972–73	45,744	25,866	—	21.8	—	—	272.70	926
1973–74	45,429	25,146	136,359	21.3	333.2	3,182	277.59	924
1974–75	45,053	24,560	—	20.8	—	—	294.04	906
1975–76	44,791	24,718	141,944	20.4	315.6	3,329	300.34	903
1976–77	44,317	24,761	—	20.3	—	3,367	301.05	899
1977–78	43,577	24,668	—	19.7	—	3,478	333.53	897
1978–79	42,550	23,877	159,000	19.3	267.6	3,510	349.59	894
1979–80	41,645	22,386	156,166	19.1	266.7	3,492	347.92	890
1980–81	40,987	22,169	165,140	19.0	248.2	3,470	325.51	890
1981–82	40,099	22,284	—	18.9	—	3,465	255.16	893
1982–83	39,652	22,946	183,826	18.8	215.7	3,580	252.34	893
1983–84	39,352	23,432	—	18.5	—	3,742	252.16	897
1984–85	39,293	24,280	189,456	18.1	207.4	3,848	252.39	906
1985–86	39,513	25,313	191,660	17.9	206.2	4,051	267.09	906
1986–87	39,712	26,119	—	18.0	—	—	—	—

SOURCE: Digest of Education Statistics, 1987.

a. Enrollment in educational institutions, U.S. public schools, K–12, 1960–86 (table 2, p. 8).
b. Estimated average annual salary of teachers in public elementary and secondary schools, constant 1985–86 dollars (table 51, p. 61).
c. Officials and administrators at schools and school districts, statistics of state school systems 1975–76, constant 1985–86 dollars, statistics of public elementary and secondary school systems.
d. Public school elementary and secondary pupil-teacher ratios, U.S. 1960–86 (table 46, p. 57).
e. Public school elementary and secondary administrator pupil ratios.
f. Total expenditure (federal, state, and local) per pupil in average daily attendance in public elementary and secondary schools; U.S., 1960–86; constant 1985–86 dollars (table 98, p. 112).
g. Federal expenditures per pupil; constant 1985–86 dollars (consumer price index, table 93, p. 107).
h. Scholastic Aptitude Test score averages for college-bound high school seniors; U.S., 1960–86 (table 80, p. 94).
— Data not available.

$2,997 ($3,465 in 1985–1986 constant dollars), In other words, even though from 1963 to 1981, per-student expenditures in constant dollars increased by a little more than 75 percent, and the total federal expenditures increased by 300 percent, the results were substantially worse than they had been before the significant funding increases began.

Figure 5.1 demonstrates that from 1963 to 1981, for every dollar increase in spending, there was a corresponding decline in quality as measured by the national average SAT score. Some would argue that this is the result of our testing a wider range of students during the period subsequent to 1963.

Unfortunately, this argument is negated by the fact that the total number of individuals as well as the percentage of individuals scoring in the higher ranges also declined during the same period. Clearly, the fact that more individuals were tested shouldn't adversely affect the number or percentage of individuals who tested in the top scoring range. In addition, the SAT scores mentioned are averages of college-bound high school students, *and* of high school students in general. Including all high school students would only reduce those averages even more. The inescapable conclusion is that educational quality has declined in direct proportion to increased federal control, the increased centralization of decision making, and the resulting loss of control by local officials and, most importantly, parents.

A Curious Reversal

It's significant that during the Reagan Administration, when the growth curve of federal expenditures for education declined somewhat, SAT scores actually improved for the first time in seventeen years.

By 1986, the average SAT score increased to 906, 431 on verbals and 475 on math. In fact, the average SAT scores have either improved or remained constant in each year of the Reagan Administration. In

FIGURE 5.2
EXPENDITURES AND RATIONS FOR PUBLIC COLLEGES AND UNIVERSITIES

School Year	Fall Undergrad. (in thou.)[a]	Expend. per Student (con. '85–86 $)[b]	Fall Faculty (in thou.)[c]	Avg. Fac. Salary (con. '85–86 $)[d]	Faculty/ Pupil Ratio[e]
1959–60	3,365*	—	—	—	—
1960–61	—	—	—	—	—
1961–62	3,861*	—	—	—	—
1962–63	—	—	—	—	—
1963–64	4,495*	—	—	—	—
1964–65	—	—	—	—	—
1965–66	5,526*	—	—	—	—
1966–67	—	—	—	—	—
1967–68	6,406*	—	—	—	—
1968–69	—	—	—	—	—
1969–70	—	—	—	—	—
1970–71	7,376	9,641	474	—	15.6
1971–72	7,743	9,410	492	—	15.8
1972–73	7,941	9,632	500	35,205	15.9
1973–74	8,261	9,619	527	—	15.7
1974–75	8,798	9,658	567	—	15.5
1975–76	9,679	9,853	628	32,631	15.4
1976–77	9,429	9,706	633	—	14.9
1977–78	9,714	9,699	678	—	14.3
1978–79	9,691	10,011	—	—	—
1979–80	9,998	10,061	675	29,951	14.8
1980–81	10,475	9,836	686	29,278	15.3
1981–82	10,755	9,603	705	29,424	15.3
1982–83	10,825	9,667	—	30,147	—
1983–84	10,846	9,831	723	—	15.0
1984–85	10,618	10,348	—	31,331	—
1985–86	10,597	—	710	32,392	14.9
1986–87	10,724†	—	698‡	—	—

SOURCE: Digest of Education Statistics, 1987.

a. Total undergraduate enrollment in institutions of higher education: U.S., fall 1969–85.
b. Expenditures per full-time equivalent student in institutions of higher education, by type and control of institutions: U.S. 1970–71 through 1984–85.
c. Full-time and part-time senior instruction staff in institutions of higher education, U.S. fall 1970–86.
d. Average salary of full-time instructional faculty in institutions of higher education. U.S. 1972–83 to 1985–86.
e. Same as b and d.
— Data not available.

NOTE: Faculty also teaches graduate and professional students.

*Includes all students enrolled in programs creditable toward a bachelor's or higher degree.
†Preliminary data.
‡Estimates.

contrast, the average SAT scores declined in each year of the Carter Administration when federal spending for education was increasing dramatically.

Does the gradual improvement in SAT scores under the Reagan Administration demonstrate that it's the increase or decrease in federal dollars spent on education that has caused the decline or improvement in the quality of public education? Of course not. What it does demonstrate is that with a relative decrease in federal financing of education and the corresponding decrease in federal *control* under the Reagan Administration, there has been a corresponding increase in the quality of public education. The cause is often incorrectly attributed to money rather than policy control.

President Reagan's Policy Changes Responsible for Recent Gains

President Reagan and the two secretaries of education who have served under him have repeatedly stated their intentions to return control of the public education system to parents and local school officials. This is the only way to achieve greater responsiveness from an otherwise rigid and immovable bureaucracy. Although their promise and subsequent satisfaction of that promise have been met by the loud disapproval of the education bureaucracy and the National Education Association, the positive results of the decision are undeniable. Not surprisingly, the same individuals and groups that have been critical of the education policy changes made by the Reagan Administration deny that the shift toward local control has had anything to do with the improved test scores. They argue that these changes would have occurred anyway. However, you can bet that if quality had *declined* rather than improved under the Reagan Administration, these same critics would have been the first to blame the downswing on the Reagan Administration's policies.

In short, it is not mere coincidence that during the same period that average SAT scores have risen, we have begun to reverse the trend of increasing federal control of our primary and secondary education systems. As a result, parents and local school boards are beginning to exercise more decision-making control over their own policies. As positive as these recent changes have been, however, much remains to be done. Regrettably, the amount of federal control over local education policy is still far too much compared to the overall contribution of federal financial funding. On average, state and local governments provide 92 percent of all funding for public schools. State and local governments, however, determine far less than 92 percent of the education policy.

DECLINE BEFORE THE REAGAN ADMINISTRATION

Because there are those who want to regress to the failed education policies of the past, it is important to examine and understand the extent that the quality of public education had declined before President Reagan took office. The magnitude of the decline in the quality of public education prior to the beginning of the Reagan Administration and its effect on our nation's future have been addressed by several recent studies. In its 1982 report titled "A Nation at Risk," the product of President Reagan's Commission on Education, the National Commission on Excellence concluded as follows:

> While we can take justifiable pride in what our schools and colleges have historically accomplished and contributed to the United States and the well-being of its people, the educational foundations of our society are presently being eroded by a rising tide of mediocrity that threatens our very future as a Nation and a people. What was unimaginable a generation ago had begun to occur. Others are matching and surpassing our educational achievement.

The Commission further concluded:

> If an unfriendly power had attempted to impose on America the mediocre education performance that exists today, we might have viewed it as an act of war. As it stands, we have allowed it to happen to ourselves. We have, in effect, been committing an act of unthinking, unilateral educational disarmament.

That same commission documented its conclusions with the following concrete examples:

> Some 23 million adults are functionally illiterate by the simplest test of everyday reading, writing, and comprehension.
>
> About 13 percent of all 17-year-olds in the United States can be considered functionally illiterate. Functional illiteracy among minority youth may run as high as 40 percent.
>
> Average achievement of high school students on most standardized tests is now lower than 26 years ago when Sputnik was launched.
>
> The College Board's Scholastic Aptitude Test, SATs, demonstrate a virtually unbroken decline from 1963 to 1980. Average verbal scores fell over 50 points and average mathematics scores dropped nearly 40 points.
>
> Both the number and proportion of students demonstrating superior achievement on SATs (i.e. those with scores of 650 or higher) have also dramatically declined.
>
> Many 17-year-olds do not possess the "higher order" intellectual skills we should expect from them. Nearly 40 percent cannot draw inferences from written material; only one-fifth can write persuasive essays, and only one-third can solve

the mathematics problems requiring several steps.

After citing these examples, the Commission concluded:

> Each generation of Americans has outstripped its parents in education, in literacy and in economic attainment. For the first time in the history of our country, the educational skills of one generation will not surpass, will not equal, will not even approach those of their parents.

Another commission report, written by the Carnegie Commission, reached similar conclusions with respect to the mediocrity of American education.

THE CONSTITUTION AND EDUCATION

An article that appeared February 15, 1987, in *The Atlanta Journal & Constitution* offers new insight into why we have experienced so many problems in our public and private education system. The article cited a New Orleans-based poll of 1,004 Americans that showed that only a bare majority knew the purpose of the 200-year-old document known as our Constitution; 59 percent were unaware that the Bill of Rights consists of the first ten amendments to the Constitution; and nearly half believed that the Constitution contains the Marxist declaration, "From each according to his ability; to each according to his need."[1]

This poll indicates that far too few Americans are knowledgeable about our Constitution. It's no wonder, then, that even fewer understand its original intent with respect to who ought to bear primary responsibility for educating our children. Nowhere in the four corners of the Constitution is there any justification for the federal government to be involved in educational policy.

Education at the Constitutional Convention

The history of the Constitutional Convention indicates that the Framers were consciously aware of this restraint, inasmuch as several of them specifically tried to place federal authority and jurisdiction over education into the Constitution.

On May 29, 1787, for example, Charles Pinckney presented in his draft constitution a power in the U.S. Legislature to "establish and provide for a national university at the seat of government of the United States."[2] When the committee that considered the matter reported their constitutional draft on August 6, 1787, they completely excluded the provision Pinckney had suggested.

Later in the convention, on August 18, James Madison and others proposed several items to be included within the legislative power of the United States, including the power "to establish a university." This provision was also rejected. Then on September 14, Madison and Pinckney, during debates on yet another draft they had submitted, moved to vest Congress with power "to establish a university, in which no preferences or distinctions should be allowed on account of religion." The proposal was again defeated on a vote by the Convention as a whole. On September 17, the Constitution, void of any congressional power over education, was ratified.

EARLY PRESIDENTIAL PROPOSALS

Washington's Proposal

In his first inaugural address, President Washington once again addressed the issue of establishing a national university. When the first Congress convened in New York, it considered his proposal and concluded that it was unconstitutional.

Jefferson's Proposal

More than fifteen years later, on March 4, 1805, in his second inaugural address, President Thomas Jefferson proposed yet another approach to establishing federal involvement in education. His plan, referring to revenue contributions on the conscription of foreign articles, was as follows:

> These contributions enable us to support the current expenses of the Government . . . and to apply such a surplus to our public debt and that redemption, once effected the revenue thereby liberated may, by a just repartition of it among the States and a corresponding amendment of the Constitution, be applied in time of peace to . . . education, and other great objects within each state.[3]

Later, in his sixth annual address to the Congress, on December 2, 1806, President Jefferson made the following statement regarding education:

> I suppose an amendment to the Constitution, by consent of the States, necessary, because the objects now recommended are not among those enumerated in the Constitution, and to which it permits the public monies to be applied.[4]

Madison's Proposal

After James Madison became president, he again tried to establish a federally funded, national university. In his inaugural address, Madison acknowledged it would require a constitutional amendment for Congress to assume any jurisdiction in the area of education.

Time after time after time in the first 100 years of our history, the Congress considered the issue of federal involvement in education and on each occasion reached the conclusion that, without first passing a constitutional amendment, they were without authority to assume any jurisdiction over the responsibility for financing education or establishing educational policy. While educating the citizens was clearly a priority, these early statesmen clearly understood that it was uniquely within the authority and responsibility of the states and individuals.

THE POINT OF DEPARTURE

It wasn't until 1866 and 1867 that we began to see a significant departure from this well established constitutional view. Specifically, on June 5, 1866, a proposal was offered in the U.S. House of Representatives to establish under the Department of the Interior, a Bureau of Education. The stated purpose of the bureau was, according to General James Garfield (who was later to become the twentieth President of the United States), to collect "such statistics and facts as shall show the condition and progress of education in the several states and territories."[5]

In speaking against the proposal, Andrew Jackson Rogers, a Representative from New Jersey, argued that if the federal government once established jurisdiction in the area of education, federal control over education would necessarily follow. In his statement on the floor of the House, he made the following point:

> [The bill] proposes to put under the supervision of a bureau established at Washington all the schools and educational institutions of the different States of the Union by collecting such facts

and statistics as will warrant them by amendments here after to the law now attempted to be passed, to control and regulate thè educational system of the whole country.[6]

Rogers concluded that such a bureau was contrary to the Founding Fathers' intent and the express language of the Constitution, and that it could not be done constitutionally without first passing an amendment authorizing such federal jurisdiction. The final portion of Roger's speech against the establishment of a Bureau of Education was much more than an argument; it was, in fact, prophetic:

> No man can find anywhere in the letter or spirit of the Constitution one word that will authorize the Congress of the United States to establish an Education Bureau. If Congress has the right to establish an Education Bureau . . . for the purpose of collecting statistics and controlling the schools of the country, then by the same parity of reason, a fortiori, Congress has the right to establish a bureau to supervise the education of all the children that are to be found in . . . this country. You will not stop at simply establishing a bureau for the purpose of paying officers to collect and diffuse statistics in reference to education.[7]

A New Bureau Created

Despite Representative Roger's argument, his colleagues failed to adhere to the intent of the Framers, and the bureau was created with no constitutional basis. More than a hundred years later, in 1979, the Congress took another giant step further away from maintaining local control and passed a bill establishing a separate agency, the Department of Education, and a separate cabinet-level post, the Secretary of Education, to oversee the activities and policies of that agency.

The extent to which we have abandoned our Constitution's original intent can be seen by the fact that in the debate to establish the Department of Education, unlike the debate to establish the Bureau of Education, very little attention was focused on the constitutionality of such a federal department. Rather, the debate was about how much it would cost and exactly what administrative powers the agency would have. We have certainly, for the sake of expediency, sacrificed our personal rights over this crucial area, and just as importantly, unconstitutionally rewritten the Constitution of the United States.

WHOSE RESPONSIBILITY?

Because of our ignorance and lack of knowledge about the content of the Constitution and the philosophical foundation that undergirds it, we have failed to adhere to its tenets, and in so doing have allowed our educational system to deteriorate. By ignoring the clear intent of the Constitution to leave the responsibility of education to the family, church, and state and local governments, we have not only weakened our educational system, but we've also unnecessarily created numerous divisive issues that we're now trying with little success to solve. These issues include school prayer, equal access, sex education, creationism, textbook content, observance of religious holidays, and whether and whose values ought to be taught.

The bedrock belief of our Founders was that the responsibility for educating a child, including the responsibility of transmitting basic values and beliefs, rests with the child's parents rather than the state. This concept is, of course, diametrically opposed to that embraced by some past civilizations such as the ancient Greek democracies, which assumed that children were the wards of the state. In the Greek model, it was the responsibility of the state to transmit the state's values to the children, even if those values differed from the values of the parents. Nor was this concept unique to ancient Greece. Adolf Hitler used the same premise in establishing the Hitler Youth. Are we to be guilty of following the same concept?

WHOSE VALUES?

By recognizing parental responsibility and the right of parents to teach and train their children in their own values rather than the values of the state, the Constitution assures religious freedom and pluralism. Today, however, we have established a monopolistic public school system that seeks to transmit values upon which the educational experts can agree. All too frequently, the values transmitted conflict with the values of the parents. Is it not surprising, therefore, that one of the hottest topics of debate today is the question of whether values ought to be taught in our primary and secondary schools.

The fact that we're even debating such an issue indicates how severe our real problem in America is. More and more educational experts are now openly admitting that values must be taught in public schools. This is apparently an admission that the prevalent attitude of the 1970s that everyone ought to be free to do his own thing hasn't been working.

America is not alone in this dilemma. Other countries face exactly the same problem. Israel, for instance, is one country that has successfully addressed the problem. When I visited Israel in August of 1987, I had the privilege of meeting with the Mayor of Tel Aviv. During the course of our meeting I asked how his government has dealt with the issue of value transmission in its public schools, given the fact that the city of Tel Aviv has an extremely diverse population consisting of virtually every denomination of Christianity, various Muslim sects, and orthodox, as well as nonorthodox Jews.

He explained that in Tel Aviv parents are free to choose from a variety of religious and nonreligious schools, all of which are financed by the government. Under their system, religious Jews may send their children to any of a number of Hebrew schools, religious Christians may send their children to any of a variety of Christian schools, and religious Muslims may send their children to any of the numerous Muslim schools. Nonreligious parents may send their children to any of the government-funded nonsectarian schools. According to the Mayor, this approach has resulted in quality schools and pluralism and is a sensible solution to the question of whose values ought to be taught in schools financed by the public.

In effect, Tel Aviv's public education system allows parents to choose the schools their children attend while at the same time providing government payment for their children's education. Tel Aviv's system proves that quality public education, pluralism, and parental values need not be mutually exclusive.

It's amazing that it's taken so long to rediscover how impossible it is to teach in a moral vacuum. Now that we're engaged in this debate, however, the only question appears to be whose values ought to be taught. The answer ought to be the values of the parents. Unfortunately, this is not the case. Too frequently, textbooks and teachers stray from teaching ethics and integrity and instead try to remove all values whatsoever.

THE POLITICIZATION OF THE CLASSROOM

Another major problem in education today is the failure to teach the facts in an unbiased and straightforward fashion. Frequently, teachers themselves are totally unaware that rather than teaching the facts and letting the student reach his or her own conclusion, they actually editorialize and, in the process, omit significant facts. The following example illustrates this problem. In my last race for Congress, I was engaged in a candidate debate in a high school in my district. The debate was designed for the students', not the faculty's, participation. During the course of the debate, however, one teacher raised her hand. Her question was, "Congressman Swindall, what is your opinion of Star Wars? What is your position on it?"

I said, "I think it's a fine movie."

Visibly perturbed, she responded, "What are you talking about? I asked your opinion of Star Wars."

I said, "The only 'Star Wars' with which I am familiar is a movie by that name."

At that point she said, "You know what I'm talking about, I'm talking about the whole notion of the Reagan Administration to bring war into space."

I replied, "I think what you are referring to is the Strategic Defense Initiative (SDI) and the reason I didn't respond to you the first time is that you were in essence editorializing when you asked the question as you did about my position on 'Star Wars.' This happens to be a government class, and it seems to me that the students here would be much better served if you used correct nomenclature rather than embracing the nomenclature of individuals who are opposed to the president's initiative and who through various editorial opinions have dubbed the Strategic Defense Initiative as 'Star Wars.' To embrace the term 'Star Wars' is to concede, incorrectly I might add, that SDI is an offensive rather than a defensive system." I then went on to state that I was supportive of the president's initiative. But my real point was that teachers ought to try to present important ideas and issues without their own political bias.

Even when they try to teach the facts and avoid editorializing, however, a certain degree of it is inevitable. But the problem it presents has increased significantly as the public schools have moved away from teaching children how to read, write, and compute and deliberately begun to editorialize about politics and secular values. The example of the teacher's bias against the Strategic Defense Initiative is typical. In fact, the teacher's position is consistent with the political positions of the NEA.

There are other problems resulting from the removal of educational decisions from local control. Washington bureaucrats, caught up in issues separate and oftentimes irrelevant to local school interests, take control and skew priorities, much to the detriment of our children's educational benefits. The NEA is one such organization that, under the guise of promoting better education, in fact wields power for their own political causes and contributes largely to the federal bureaucratic control of our educational system.

An examination of just a few of the items on the NEA's extensive legislative agenda brings additional understanding of the problem. In its printed agenda adopted in July 1986, the NEA listed among other positions the following:

- NEA opposes any constitutional amendment respecting tax limitations or the federal budget;
- NEA supports a mutual, verifiable nuclear freeze with cessation of testing, production and a further deployment of nuclear delivery systems and other destablizing systems;
- NEA opposes weakening national security by decreasing federal funding for education while disproportionately increasing the defense budget;
- NEA opposes the use of vouchers in education;
- NEA opposes "choice" in education programs which supplants or reduces existing [federal] funding levels for public education programs; . . .

- NEA opposes US military or economic aid to governments permitting violations of their citizens' rights.

These are but a few of the more than 200 specific political issues covered by the NEA's legislative agenda. Other issues range from opposition to tax indexing to recognizing the rights of homosexuals. To achieve its left-wing political agenda, the NEA regularly lobbies Congress and expends millions of dollars on congressional and presidential candidates who support its views.

One of the NEA's key issues in the ninety-ninth Congress was sanctions against South Africa. Any member of Congress who voted against such sanctions, regardless of his or her reasons, was rated as being "opposed to education." To say the least, the NEA has a political agenda that extends far beyond basic education issues. And unfortunately for public education in America, the union's agenda is in too many cases adversely affecting the objective nature of classroom instruction that quality education requires. In a paper entitled "The Politicization of the Classroom," written by Marcella D. Hadeed for inclusion in the book *A Blueprint for Education Reform*, Mrs. Hadeed summarized the problem presented by a politicized classroom:

> "Totalitarian regimes have long recognized the teacher's power to mold ideas, influence behavior, and shape belief. That is why their schools are integral parts of the government control apparatus. . . ." Chester E. Finn
>
> According to Chester E. Finn, "one of the abiding strengths of American education . . . is that we have not politicized the classroom, or turned teachers into propagandists, or willfully instructed our children through curricula that seek to indoctrinate." For Americans, education is learning to read, to write and to compute. Educa-

tion is the transmittal of knowledge of history, philosophy, literature, science and art . . . of Western culture. Students learn to reason and analyze and make judgments. According to Edwin J. DeLattre, President of St. John's College, "the first and most fundamental feature of education worthy of the name is that it promotes aspiration in the young, that is, it promotes the desire to become more and better than one is. The encouragement of aspiration depends, above all, on both intellectual and moral propagation."

Quietly and ominously, however, politics is creeping into the once sacrosanct American classroom. It does not appear in the form of one more fad on an already bloated list of electives from which young groping minds must select a certain total in order to obtain their diplomas. If it were that isolated and easily identified, astute students who are hungry for substance and truth in education could avoid it. Neither is it only a distorted version of the course we once knew as U.S. Government. The politics to which I refer is an increasing presence, brought about by the implantation of dogma spun by liberal ideologues, which permeate education like a poisonous vapor. Unless immediate and courageous reforms are courageously undertaken to stop the process, the gradual politicization of the classroom instruction will have a cumulative and corruptive effect on American education that, in time, will permanently alter American society in ways that will infringe on individual freedom and our right to the pursuit of happiness.

The politicization of American education is subtle compared to a totalitarian state. The means used to achieve this end are what one might expect, however: curricula and teachers.

Evidence of this phenomenon can be seen in changes in textbooks over the last 15–20 years and the change in attitude of the largest teachers' union, the National Education Association. For example, in public school textbooks, author Frances Fitzgerald (no conservative) discovered, "there is either no past, no history at all—only 'social studies' and 'current events,' or else a pot/pourri of 'pasts,' each tied to some current theme such as ethnicity, sexuality, or politics." Mary Futrell, President of NEA, speaking at the 1982 NEA convention (then NEA-union secretary-treasurer) said, "there's no alternative to political involvement. Instruction and professional development (of teachers) have been on the back burner to us compared to political action."

In the past 15–20 years, curricula in the schools have been diluted—geography and history have become "social studies," civics has become "contemporary world problems" and American Government is taught, in many cases, with biased textbooks.[8]

So long as this type of politicization continues in public education, the necessity for parental choice in the schools their children attend becomes even more crucial. By allowing the same type of choice in primary and secondary education that now exists in higher education, some of the problems can be corrected.

THE HIGHER EDUCATION SYSTEM IN CONTRAST

The higher education system, which has been controlled by the pressures of free enterprise and choice, stands in stark contrast to the primary and secondary public education monopoly. Rather than experiencing the huge increases in administrators-per-pupil ratios or the huge increases in per-student expenditures that have characterized our elementary and high school public education system, during the same time period from 1963–1983, the higher education system experienced virtually no increase in per-student, constant-dollar expenditures or administrators-per-student ratios. During the same time period, one can no doubt conclude that American colleges and universities have maintained a consistently high level of quality.

In 1970, for example, the first year complete data for primary and secondary and higher education are available, per-student expenditures for public elementary and secondary schools in the United States were $1,049 ($2,874 in constant 1985–86 dollars) as compared with $3,740 in 1984 ($3,848 in constant 1985–86 dollars), up nearly 34 percent. In contrast, in 1970 the per-student expenditures for public colleges and universities were, in constant 1985–86 dollars, $9,641 as compared with $10,348 for 1984, up 7 percent. While the cost in constant dollars of postsecondary education is no doubt higher than elementary and secondary expenses, these figures are shown to demonstrate the increase in per-student expenditures that have characterized our present primary and secondary system. These substantial percentage increases have not occurred in the higher education system where "cost containment" is achieved as a result of free-enterprise constraints and the pressures of choice and competition among the schools that comprise the higher education system.

Choice at the College Level

When parents and students choose their college or university, they almost always consider the reputation of the institution and its faculty. Is it liberal or conservative, strict or lax in discipline, and so on? Frequently, the parents and student visit the faculty, the administration, and the campus to find out what type of philosophical twist the administration and faculty are placing on their instruction. This is certainly valid, because parents *ought* to be concerned about what their children are going to be taught. And if it's valid at the college level, isn't it equally, or even more valid at the elementary and high school levels, where the students are younger and more impressionable?

If parental values are to survive the onslaught presented by the liberal educational establishment in Washington, a solution similar to the one afforded by choice is essential. Aside from the increase in efficiency and cost effectiveness, choice will minimize the conflict that now exists between the rights of parents to transmit their values to their children and the schools' desire not to offend the students (or parents of the students) whom they must teach. Without a system that allows parents a choice in the values that are taught to their children, this inevitable conflict will continue.

Parents who have values and religious beliefs that are different from the majority or are unacceptable to the intellectual elite ought not to be required to compromise their values in order to take advantage of that portion of their tax dollars spent on education. Yet that is exactly what our current system is forcing them to do. If parents don't approve of the values that are being transmitted in public schools, they are told in essence that they ought to send their children to a private school. But the problem with this approach is that if parents choose the private school option, they are, in effect, required to pay twice. They pay once when they pay their taxes, and again when they pay their child's private school tuition.

RETHINKING THE ENTIRE SYSTEM

Rather than continuing to attempt to find solutions within a system that literally defies such solutions, perhaps it is time to reexamine the system itself.

We *can* find meaningful solutions to the many educational issues that divide our nation today. Such solutions will be found, however, only if we're willing to reexamine our current system with an understanding that the conclusion may be that the system itself is the source of many of our problems. To date we have failed to clearly establish educational quality as our primary objective, because the very individuals responsible for establishing and operating the current system now have a vested interest in maintaining that system as it is.

I first realized this when I sponsored the TEACH bill in 1985. Shortly after I sponsored the bill, numerous administrators and spokespersons for the NEA accused me and other sponsors of wanting to undermine public education. Such an accusation was and is illogical because my proposal was to *reform,* not eliminate, public education. Again, I would like to mention that the bill proposed a trial project on one specific federal program. It would not have closed down the public schools, nor would we have witnessed a flood of withdrawals from the system. But were parents given the choice, I think we would have seen greater accountability and partnership between parents and educators in the programs—resulting is better education for our youth. And isn't that our ultimate goal? To refuse to try viable alternatives to the current system for the exclusive purpose of maintaining the current public school *system* is, in my opinion, a distortion of priorities and a failure to act responsibly. This is the attitude, I feel, we have fallen into, and it has come at a tremendous cost, both in the billions of dollars of taxpayers' money that has been misspent, as well as in the educational benefits denied our children.

The NEA's accusation was analogous to accusing someone of being opposed to the defense of our country simply because that person dared to offer a bill to reform the Pentagon. In essence, these individuals were contending that unless you support the public school system *as they have established and developed it,* you not only "don't support public education," but you're actually out to undermine it.

It's a common tactic of many today to assert that if you don't support a federal solution to a problem, especially *their* proposed program, you don't want to solve the problem at all, or you're insincere about helping others. Thus, the comments by the spokesperson for the NEA are understandable only if you realize that their union wants to protect the system it has helped establish and develop.

Parents Want Choice

Many polls have shown that Americans have a growing interest in and support for increased freedom of choice by parents in matters of education. A recent Gallup–Phi Delta Kappa poll shows that a majority of American parents (56 percent) prefers private schools to government schools. Forty-nine percent of parents whose children are now in public schools say they would send their children to private schools if they had tuition assistance. Other recent surveys, including one conducted among public school teachers in Chicago, show that public school teachers are twice as likely to send their own children to private schools as are parents in the general population. Do they know something that the general public doesn't?

In a recent poll in Louisiana, almost six out of every ten people favored vouchers, with women more in favor than men, blacks more than whites, low-income parents more than the wealthier, those with the most-recent experience in the schools more than older people, and those with school-aged children more than those without. This follows the national trend lines as well, and it shows clearly that there's a strong and growing sentiment in our nation for educational freedom and choice. Americans do not like being locked into a centralized system with little or no freedom of choice, and with little or no influence over key educational decisions. This is true in part because parents know that as their ability to influence the decision-making process has diminished, so, too, has their ability to solve the unique problems of our situation.

Teachers and Defense Contractors

For spokespersons of the teachers' union to oppose competition in public education is as predictable as major defense contractors' opposing competition in bidding for defense contracts. Of course a defense contractor would prefer not to have to bid in competition with others. Defense contractors inevitably argue that they welcome the competition, but because their experience gives them unique knowledge and ability, they alone can build the product in a quality fashion. Usually, however, such quality will cost twice as much, or more as the same goods priced competitively. And the real irony is that despite the protests of defense contractors, actual results time and again demonstrate that competition *reduces* the price, and also *improves* the quality.

Why should education be any different? Sure, many of the teachers' unions are going to continue to argue that education is different and quality would suffer in a competitive system. The fact remains, however, that the average per-pupil cost for private elementary and high school education is roughly *half* the cost in public schools, while at the same time, not surprisingly, the *quality* of private education has been proved by objective testing to be consistently *superior* to that of the public schools.

TOWARD A RESTORATION

It *is* possible to bring positive change in public education so as to restore choice, competition, and control to parents and local and state governments. But it will happen only if we are willing to examine our current system objectively, and judge it on the basis of actual results, not on the basis of future results or how well-intended past policymakers have been. Such an objective examination will inevitably lead to reform and restoration of quality and parental rights.

Starting with the Constitution

The starting point in this examination and restoration process is, once again, the Constitution. The Constitution correctly places the responsibility for financing education and establishing educational policy not in the federal government, but rather at the state, local, and family levels. By recognizing the wisdom of the Constitution's writers in refusing any type of jurisdiction or control over education for the federal government, we can begin to restore the quality of education, strengthen the roles of families, and obtain more value for the dollars we spend.

Equally important, we can avoid many of the complex and divisive First Amendment problems that have been caused by our ignorance of the clear constitutional restraints placed on the federal government.

Federal Funding, Federal Meddling

Given the current level of federal programs and federal spending aimed at public schools, it's probably unrealistic to attempt to get the federal government out of the business of financing our public schools altogether. But it's not unrealistic to get the federal government out of public educational policy. As soon as possible, Congress must return educational policy and administration to parents and to the state and local governments, where the policy can reflect local needs and concerns. This can be done by appropriating federal funds with no strings attached. With the exception of those who operate inside the beltway surrounding Washington, D.C., few really doubt that parents, teachers, and state and local governments are far more capable of addressing their own educational policies than are bureaucrats in our nation's capital.

Once local and state authorities are freed from federal control, they may want to consider modeling their primary and secondary school systems after our private schools or our higher education system. As we've seen, the competition and choice that exist in those areas, which have remained subject to the pressures of the free enterprise system, have been healthy for the schools and students alike. Similar pressures and restraints would improve public education at the primary and secondary levels as well.

The First Amendment problems that have plagued our public education system have been significantly less problematic in our colleges and universities, and virtually nonexistent in our private elementary and high schools. This is because parents are free to choose the schools their children attend. They are also free to choose the values that are transmitted.

Even our system of higher education could be in trouble, however, if the courts continue the recent trend of federal encroachment represented by the cases of Bob Jones University and Grove City College. But thus far our higher education system has provided an excellent model with a proven track record. Why not use it as a starting point for revamping our current primary and secondary education system?

WHY THE FEDERAL GOVERNMENT TOOK OVER EDUCATION

In constructively analyzing our educational policy, it's important to recognize why the federal government increased its presence and control in the first place. It was primarily because of justified distrust of the state and local governments' willingness to redress racial prejudice and civil rights problems. Our mistake, however, was in using the Department of Education (and before its creation the Department of Health, Education, and Welfare) to attempt to achieve justice rather than using the Justice Department as our Constitution provides. Civil rights violations must be addressed at the federal level, but it's both inefficient and ineffective to use the Department of Education to attempt such a purpose, and to bring about enforcement. It's like going around the block, instead of going directly across, to get to the other side of the street. You might eventually get there, but a lot of energy and resources have been wasted in the process. In addition, the unnecessary route creates all kinds of opportunities for distractions detrimental to reaching the final goal.

By administering justice for all citizens through the proper channels of the Justice Department as our Constitution provides, we can again allow parents, teachers, and state and local governments to address educational issues. Most importantly, we can reinstate the important constitutional principle that it is the right and responsibility of a child's parents, not the state, to educate children, especially in moral, political, and economic principles.

Because education has always afforded the most direct route to economic, physical, and spiritual success, it is important that we focus as much energy and creativity as possible into restoring educational opportunity in America. For too long, we have allowed our educational system to promote the interests and objectives of the educational experts.

The educational system that once served as a melting pot and allowed the diverse members of our society to come together without having to conform to a predetermined "norm" has gradually evolved into a system that attempts to mold everyone into one secularist mind-set. The diverse values and beliefs of our nation's parents are ever slowly giving way to the values and beliefs of the state.

America's past successes have in large part resulted from the diversity and competitiveness of her people and the inability of the majority to impose its will on the minority. Our future successes depend on our ability to remain diverse and competitive. By restructuring our current educational system and returning control to parents and local governments, this can be achieved once again.

6

Symptom: A Diminishing First Amendment

*I*t's no accident that many of the most controversial, divisive, and emotionally heated issues being debated in America today arise in the context of our public education system. In effect, the American classroom has become a battleground on which most First Amendment battles are now being fought. In the past several years, the Supreme Court has been called upon to decide issue after issue regarding the First Amendment rights of students and their parents. These conflicts are inevitable because the First Amendment contains two fundamental guarantees that invariably come in conflict when applied to our schools. The first guarantee is that Congress "shall make no law respecting an establishment of religion." The second guarantee is that Congress shall make no law "prohibiting the free exercise" of religion. By virtue of the Fourteenth Amendment, the restrictions on Congress have been extended to the states.

CONFUSION OF COURT DECISIONS

The various Supreme Court decisions regarding these two, often-conflicting guarantees haven't come close to settling the issues.

Zorach v. Clausen

In 1952, the Court held in *Zorach* v. *Clausen* that the New York system, in which "the public schools do no more than accommodate their schedules to a program of outside religious instruction," did not violate the First Amendment prohibition against establishing a religion. In so holding, Justice William O. Douglas stated that "we cannot read into the Bill of Rights . . . a philosophy of hostility to religion."[1]

Engel v. Vitale

Ten years later, in the *Engel* v. *Vitale* case, the Court held that a prayer required by the New York Board of Regents was unconstitutional because such an officially established prayer violated the "establishment of religion" clause of the First Amendment.[2]

Abington v. Schempp

A year later, in 1963, the Supreme Court in *Abington School District* v. *Schempp* held a state of Pennsylvania law calling for "at least ten verses from the Holy Bible shall be read, without comment, at the opening of each public school on each school day" to be an unconstitutional establishment of religion. In so holding, the Court stated that the "establishment of religion" and "free exercise" clauses require the government to be strictly neutral in matters of religion, "protecting all, preferring none, disparaging to none."[3]

Lemon v. Kurtzman

In 1971, Chief Justice Warren Burger, writing for the majority of the Court in the case of *Lemon* v. *Kurtzman,* developed guidelines for making decisions about controversies over religion and education. These guidelines are known as the "Lemon test" because they were established in the *Lemon* case. According to the Lemon test, for a law involving religion in public schools to avoid violating the Constitution, it must satisfy the following requirements:

 1. The primary purpose of the law must be *secular,* not religious. This means it must not have a religious purpose.

 2. The principle, or primary, effect of the law must not be to advance or inhibit religion.

 3. The law must not create an excessive government entanglement with religion.[4]

Wallace v. Jaffree

Even with the guidelines spelled out in the Lemon test, much confusion remains with regard to the First Amendment's application to public schools. Applying this test in the summer of 1985, the majority in the *Wallace* v. *Jaffree* decision declared unconstitutional an Alabama law that required a period of silence "for meditation or voluntary prayer in public schools."[5]

The majority's opinion in that case appears to contradict the view of at least some of the Founders when considered in light of language contained in a bill offered by Thomas Jefferson when he served in the Virginia legislature. Specifically, the bill entitled "Establishing of Elementary Schools" contained the following language: "No religious reading, instruction or exercise shall be prescribed or practiced inconsistent with the tenets of any religious sect or denomination."[6]

Jefferson's views in this area are important, because it was he who first used the phrase "wall of separation between church and state." Jefferson used his newly coined phrase in a private letter to a Baptist church in Danbury, Connecticut, that had expressed concerns about the newly formed federal government's interfering with their church's government and operation. In his letter, dated January 1802, Jefferson assured the members of the church that their fears were unfounded because there existed a wall of separation between the church and state that would absolutely prohibit the federal government from becoming involved in the affairs of the church. The letter was silent regarding the church's involvement in the affairs of the federal government.

The Alabama "Moment of Silence" legislation would certainly appear to be consistent with Jefferson's understanding of the First Amendment. And Chief Justice Burger apparently agreed, because he dissented in the *Wallace* v. *Jaffree* decision. In his dissent, Burger summarized the current dilemma regarding our public school system and the rights secured by the First Amendment:

> Some who trouble to read the opinions in this case will find it ironic—perhaps even bizarre—that on the very day we heard arguments in this case, the Court's session opened with an invocation for Divine protection. Across the park a few hundred yards away, the House of Representatives and the Senate regularly open each session with a prayer. These legislative prayers are not just one minute in duration, but are extended, thoughtful invocations and prayers for Divine guidance. They are given, as they have been since 1789, by clergy appointed as official Chaplains and paid from the Treasury of the United States. Congress has also provided chapels in the Capitol, at public expense, where Members and others may pause for prayer, meditation—or a moment of silence.
>
> Inevitably, some wag is bound to say that the Court's holding today reflects a belief that the historic practice of the Congress and this Court is justified because members of the Judiciary and Congress are more in need of Divine guidance than are schoolchildren. Still others will say that all this controversy is "much ado about noth-

ing," since no power on earth—including this Court and Congress—can stop any teacher from opening the school day with a moment of silence for pupils to meditate, to plan their day—or to pray if they voluntarily elect to do so. I make several points about today's curious holding.

It makes no sense tŏ say that Alabama has "endorsed prayer" by merely enacting a new statute "to specify expressly that voluntary prayer is *one* of the authorized activities during a moment of silence," *ante*, at 2501 (O'Conner, J., concurring in the judgment) (emphasis added). To suggest that a moment-of-silence statute that includes the word "prayer" unconstitutionally endorses religion, while one that simply provides for a moment of silence does not, manifests not neutrality, but hostility toward religion. For decades our opinions have stated that hostility toward any religion or toward all religions is as much forbidden by the Constitution as is an official establishment of religion. The Alabama legislature has no more "endorsed" religion than a state or the Congress does when it provides for legislative chaplains, or than this Court does when it opens each session with an invocation to God. Today's decision recalls the observations of Justice Goldberg:

"[U]ntutored devotion to the concept of neutrality can lead to invocation or approval of results which partake not simply of that noninterference and noninvolvement with the religious which the Constitution commands, but of a brooding and pervasive dedication to the secular and a passive, or even active, hostility to the religious. Such results are not only not compelled by the Constitution, but, it seems to me, are prohibited by it." [*School District* v. *Schempp*, 374 U.S. 203, 306, 83 (1963) (concurring opinion).]⁷

It is becoming increasingly apparent that the more cases the Supreme Court decides regarding the First Amendment rights of students and their parents, the cloudier the issue becomes and the more the rights our Founders thought they were protecting under the First Amendment diminish.

TWO POINTS OF TENSION

Aside from the school prayer issue, there are presently at least two other important First Amendment issues that exist primarily because of the public education system we have created.

Creation v. Evolution

One such issue is the teaching of creationism as an alternative to the theory of evolution. In the case of *Edwards* v. *Aguillard,* decided on June 19, 1987, the Supreme Court considered the constitutionality of a statute passed by the state of Louisiana in 1982 requiring that creation science be given balanced treatment with the theory of evolution in the public schools of Louisiana. In its decision, the Court held the Louisiana statute to be unconstitutional because it promoted religion and had no secular purpose.

Things have certainly changed in America since Congress enacted the *Northwest Ordinance of 1787,* which contained the following article: "Religion, morality, and knowledge, being necessary to good government and the happiness of mankind, schools and the means of education shall forever be encouraged."[8]

Or consider Alexis de Tocqueville's observations in his book *Democracy in America,* written after his visit to this country in 1831: "In New England every citizen is instructed in the elements of human knowledge; he is also taught the doctrine and the evidences of his religion; he must know the history of his country and the main features of its Constitution."[9]

If the Supreme Court's holding in the Louisiana case is correct regarding the teaching of creationism, consistency requires that the teaching of the Declaration of Independence itself be banned, because it is expressly a creationist document. As quoted previously, the Declaration of Independence states, "We hold these truths to be self-evident that all men are *created* equal, that they are endowed by their *Creator* with certain unalienable rights."

How can we teach the contents of the Declaration of Independence in our public schools if we really believe that creationism ought not to be taught in our public schools? The point is, you cannot. *What was self-evident in 1776 is now unconstitutional.* The real irony of the Supreme Court's current position banning the teaching of the theory of creation alongside the theory of evolution is that it contradicts the premise that educational experts and free speech advocates defended in 1925 when the Scopes trial was in progress in Tennessee.

In that trial, more popularly known as the "monkey trial," it was argued that creationism ought not to be taught to the exclusion of evolution (as was the case at the time in most school systems) because our public schools ought to be a place where *all* theories are taught, thus allowing the students to decide for themselves which is most logical. As a result of the Scopes controversy, the teaching of evolution alongside creationism gradually became the norm.

Ever so gradually, however, we have excluded the teaching of creationism, so that now *only* the theory of evolution is taught. What happened to the notion of letting students decide for themselves which theory is most logical? Those who determined to teach evolution alone defend their decision on the grounds that evolution is exclusively a scientific theory and should not be clouded by religious speculation or consideration.

Such an argument is not only misleading, however, but patently false as well. The creationism v. evolution debate is as much a religious and political debate as it is a scientific one, because the study of politics, religion, and science share a common starting point: all must begin with some explanation of the origin of mankind. How one explains our origin has profound consequences. It is intellectually dishonest to suggest that one can discuss the theory of the origin of mankind exclusively as a scientific issue.

Mortimer Adler, in *Great Books of the Western World,* has said,

> More consequences for thought and action follow the affirmation or denial of God than from answering any other basic question. . . . The whole tenor of human life is affected by whether men regard themselves as supreme beings in the universe, or acknowledge a super-human being whom they conceive of as an object of fear or love, a force to be defied or a Lord to be obeyed. Among those who acknowledge a divinity, it matters greatly whether the divine is represented merely by the concept of God—the object of philosophical speculation—or by the living God whom men worship in all the acts of piety which comprise the rituals of religion.[10]

Whether or not there is a Creator God, therefore, is no small issue for our public schools, the main institution upon which our society relies for the shaping of young, impressionable minds. To suggest, moreover, that there can be conflicting explanations in this matter, each of which is true, is preposterous. Yet that is in essence what is being argued in the creationism versus evolution debate. The real issue in the debate is *not* whether the theory of evolution ought to be taught. Certainly the theory of evolution ought to be taught. The issue is whether the theory of evolution will be taught to the *exclusion* of other theories, because such a determination is nothing short of censorship.

Many argue that religious fundamentalists, be they Jewish, Christian, Muslim, or any other sect that adheres to a creationist viewpoint, ought not to be upset by the teaching of evolution because evolution can be explained in a way that's consistent with the existence of God. For example, they argue that God could have been responsible for the "big bang" and could have been the agent behind the evolutionary process. However, even apart from the problem that such an explanation still contradicts the explanation contained in the Bible or other holy books, the fact remains that these "religious" explanations are not taught, nor, for that matter, could they be taught under the logic of the Supreme Court in *Edwards* v. *Aguillard*. The fact that evolution may be consistent with the existence of a creator in no way changes the fact that the teaching of evolution is the teaching of religion in so far as it deals with a religious issue, the origin of man. The point is that religion and science are in certain aspects inseparable.

As a practical matter, when a student is taught in a science class that he or she evolved accidentally from an ape-like creature as the result of a random, evolutionary process that began with a "big bang," that lesson has significant consequences in the realms of politics and religion. Thus, for us to believe, as advocates of the evolution-to-the-exclusion-of-creationism approach would have us, that evolution can be taught at school without substantially interfering with what parents teach their children about religion at home is incredibly naive.

For example, a Jewish, Christian, or Muslim child who is taught by his parents at home that he was created by a personal God in accordance with the creation account set forth in Genesis is going to be understandably confused when he is taught in science class that mankind accidentally evolved from a simpler lifeform. Upon hearing this, the child might well ask the teacher how he's supposed to reconcile the differences between evolutionary theory and the biblical creation account he has been taught at home.

At that point, the teacher's response will necessarily be as much a religious one as a scientific one. Most likely that response will be, "I'm here to teach you science, and what your parents teach you at home about religion is their business." Because the child knows that there can be but one truth regarding the origin of mankind, his views about religion will undoubtedly be influenced by the teacher's attempt at an unbiased response.

Am I arguing that the teacher ought not to respond? Of course not. Am I arguing that a child ought to be protected from learning anything about the world except what his parents are willing to approve? No. What I'm arguing is that we're kidding ourselves if we think you can teach in public schools without getting into religious issues.

The point is that you can't teach in a moral and religious vacuum. What a teacher states in the context of a science lecture has religious connotations. It is, therefore, a fallacy to argue that the teaching of evolution does not advance any religious tenet while the teaching of creationism does. The point is that both theories advance religion, because the study of religion, like the study of science, begins with some type of explanation regarding the origin of mankind.

Balanced Treatment Makes Sense

This dilemma can be equitably resolved only if we recognize that teaching the theory of evolution *and* the theory of creationism—and any other theory, for that matter—makes the most sense. Public schools ought to present various theories without editorial censorship, and then let the students decide for themselves which theory they believe to be most rational. During the period immediately following the Scopes trial, that's the approach we took in our public schools. Why, then, did we change our approach? Perhaps it's because those who advocate the theory of evolution realize that it requires a great deal more faith to believe the evolution account than it does to believe the creation account.

This is especially true since the theory of evolution involves serious scientific difficulties, such as it has with the second law of thermodynamics. That natural, physical law simply states that though energy in the cosmos remains constant, the amount available to do useful work is always decreasing. Conversely, entropy, which is the measure of *un*available energy, is increasing. Everything, then, is moving toward less orderliness or greater chaos.

Stated differently, according to the second law of thermodynamics, in a natural state, the complex will break down to the simple, and the organized will become disorganized, chaotic, and random. That is why dead bodies and plant life decompose and iron rusts.

Evolution, of course, teaches exactly the opposite of this natural law. It teaches that order and complexity actually increase over time. Evolutionists often respond to this problem by stating that evolution is the "grand exception."

Because evolution, with its presumption of order and complexity, runs counter to this well-established law of science, one can certainly conclude that it takes a giant leap of blind faith to believe evolution. The miracles for which religious people who believe in them are ridiculed are nothing compared to the truly astonishing things evolutionists are required to believe happened by pure accident, against substantial evidence and contrary to known laws and processes.

Evolutionary theory faces many other problems besides its conflict with the fundamental laws of thermodynamics, and the problems it has with the fossil record are not least among them. The fact is, the fossils do not appear gradually in the fossil record, in an ascending order of complexity from single cell to man, as Darwinism presupposes. Rather, they appear suddenly in the fossil record, in a veritable explosion of complex life forms in the Cambrian period, a period which, according to the evolutionists' own system, does not begin until three-fourths of the earth's geologic history has passed.

In other words, for the first three quarters of the geologic record, there is virtually nothing. At the very least, it is void of the many, many developing, ancestral links that are required if those forms, which explode on the scene suddenly in the Cambrian era, had truly evolved over millions of preceding years. Evolutionists themselves acknowledge that this is the case with the fossil record and consider it one of the major mysteries of the history of life. I should say so! It would look, to any objective observer, more like evidence for sudden creation than for gradual evolution.

The point is that there's plenty of reason for our schools to present all sides of the issue of origins. The situation is not at all as we're told—that evolutionists have all science and fact, while creationists have all faith and no facts. There is a whole lot of believing by faith among evolutionists and a lot less fact than they would like us to think. This is acknowledged on rare occasion by secular experts, and I cite one here from a college textbook:

> Actually biologists are still as far away as they ever were in their attempts to explain how the first protoplasm originated. The evidence of those who would explain life's origin on the basis of the accidental combination of suitable chemical elements is no more tangible than that of those people who place their faith in a Divine Creation as the explanation of the development of life. Obviously, the latter have as much justification for their belief as the former.[11]

Perhaps the reason we now exclude the teaching of creationism is that those who make such policy decisions don't really want our young people to make up their own minds on this issue. Whatever the reason, the fact remains that once we deny the belief that mankind was created by God and substitute a belief that mankind evolved from simple life forms, there are profound consequences.

Social Darwinism, the dog-eat-dog approach, the survival of the fittest played out in human affairs, is one of those consequences. One monstrous example of the outworking of Darwinian thinking in society was the famous Nazi Doctor Josef Mengele, whose medical atrocities at Auschwitz are well-documented. Dr. Andreas Hillgruber, professor of history at the University of Cologne, accounts for Mengele's outlook this way:

> The focus was human genetics based on social Darwinism, which approved of sterilization and euthanasia for the sake of racial hygiene. This was put forth in genetics prior to National Socialism, and later incorporated into the barbaric race doctrine of Nazi ideology. . . . He believed until his death that he served a great cause—Hitler's effort to save humanity from degeneration through racial politics, including killing millions of allegedly inferior human beings.[12]

As Mortimer Adler said, there are profound consequences from the decision you make about whether mankind is a product of evolution or the creation of God. Mengele, quite consistently, sought to weed out the inferior flesh of humanity so the strongest would survive. If man is simply meat, you treat him a certain way; if he is the image and glory of a Creator, you treat him another way. Mengele's value system, his world view, led him to treat his fellow human beings the way he did, and he sincerely believed he was serving a great cause in doing so.

Textbooks and Curricula

The other controversial issue regarding education and the First Amendment relates to school curricula and the content of textbooks. We have a hot debate right now in Atlanta over the content of school textbooks and library books. Recently a group of parents in Gwinnett County, which is adjacent to my own district in metropolitan Atlanta, found a book that they felt was offensive, and they sought to have that particular book restricted in terms of student access—not banned. One of the portions of the book that the parents found offensive described a teenage girl masturbating.

There was a huge uproar in the Atlanta media about these parents' saying they were offended by the content of this book. They were criticized for not being more open-minded about the books to which their children are exposed as part of the educational process. The argument was that the experts—that is, certain parents, teachers, and administrators—ought to decide what type of curricula and books children study, even if these books and curricula conflict with the basic values espoused by one or several of the students' parents. In other words, they were arguing that what the parents believe must give way to the beliefs of the experts.

I find that extremely contradictory and ironic, because as discussed previously, the Supreme Court has on numerous occasions stated that parents have the right not to have their children exposed to any type of religious activity in the public schools. Such activity, whether it be prayer or Bible reading, ought to be banned. Children should be shielded from it. Thus, it is apparently okay to ban or limit access to any type of religious activity, but it is not okay to limit children's exposure to material that many parents consider to be pornographic, profane, or blasphemous. Certainly these two propositions are contradictory.

Considering the complexity of the issues presented

by the First Amendment as applied to our schools, there is no way within the confines of our present public educational system that we can justly and constitutionally resolve them. The brutal fact is that without major reform, a parent's guaranteed religious freedom will continue to run smack into the perceived need of the state schools to steer clear of religious endorsements and activities.

AN OMINOUS ALTERATION

In my view, these tensions in the schools have come about because over the years there has been a gradual alteration of the meaning of the First Amendment. This ominous alteration has changed substantially the focus of the amendment. I say it's ominous because, in the short history of our nation, the amendment has been changed from a very narrow and specific restriction on the Congress to a very broad, general restriction on the free exercise of the people. By any reckoning, that kind of inversion is very sobering.

The Original Amendment

Although the phrase "separation of church and state" occurs nowhere in either the Declaration or the Constitution, a surprising number of Americans think the First Amendment includes it. The pertinent words of the actual amendment are simple and straightforward: "Congress shall make no law respecting an establishment of religion, or prohibiting the free exercise thereof. . . ."

Despite the broad construction of the First Amendment by recent Supreme Courts, the amendment the Founders wrote with respect to religion was designed to place a check on the legislative branch of the federal government, the Congress of the United States, and to be an absolute guarantee to every individual of his right to exercise his religion as he chooses. This freedom was to be guaranteed in the context of public and private settings.

Originally, only Congress could break the First Amendment. Religious organizations couldn't break it, children praying in school couldn't break it, school athletic teams saying prayers before games couldn't break it, and it couldn't be broken by crosses, creches, or any other public display of religious belief. Only Congress, by enacting a certain kind of law, could break it. Even Congress could pray, and pay ministers to lead its prayers, as has been done since the founding of our country, without breaking the First Amendment, at least thus far.

One of the most renowned justices in the history of the Supreme Court, William O. Douglas, summarized the case against an overly broad reading of the First Amendment as it relates to the affairs of the church and state in his opinion in the *Zorach* v. *Clausen* case:

> The First Amendment, however, does not say that in every and all respects there shall be a separation of Church and State. . . . Otherwise the state and religion would be aliens to each other—hostile, suspicious and even unfriendly. . . . We are a religious people whose institutions presuppose a Supreme Being. . . . When the state encourages religious instruction or cooperates with religious authorities by adjusting the schedule of public events to sectarian needs, it follows the best of our traditions, for it then respects the religious nature of our people and accommodates the public service to their spiritual needs.[13]

The First Amendment now seems to mean not only a separation of the institution of the church from the institution of the state, but also between God and state. Such an interpretation is far from what the Founders had in mind. Consider the following remarks by George Washington in his first inaugural address in 1789:

> It would be peculiarly improper to omit, in this first official act, my fervent supplication to that Almighty Being who rules over the universe, who presides in the councils of nations, and whose providential aids can supply every human defect, that His benediction may consecrate to the liberties and happiness of the people of the United States. No people can be bound to acknowledge and adore the invisible hand which conducts the affairs of men more than the people of the United States. Every step by which they have advanced to the character of an independent nation seems to have been distinguished by some token of providential agency. . . . We ought to be no less persuaded that the propitious smiles of Heaven can never be expected on a nation that disregards the eternal rules of order and right, which Heaven itself has ordained.[14]

If we were guided by what the Founders meant, we would only worry about the First Amendment's being broken when Congress is in session and about to make a law that has to do with an establishment of religion. We wouldn't worry about it when evangelical voters exercised their political rights, or when any other religious person acted politically in some fashion. We wouldn't worry about its being broken by churches, synagogues, chaplains, ministers, prayer groups in schools, or even the president.

The Separation Replacement

As we all know, however, that is precisely the vein in which we worry most about the First Amendment today. How did this happen? How did it cease being a check on what kind of laws Congress could make with respect to religion and become instead a check on what kind of public religious activity in which the people could engage? Was there an amendment to change it in this way? Was there opportunity for the people to discuss changing it to mean this, to have their elected representatives vote on the new proposal so that it would become part of their fundamental law?

No, none of these things has occurred. No legal, constitutionally authorized means has been employed to alter the First Amendment in this fundamental way. It has been changed gradually throughout our national history, as Congress and the Courts have followed a checkered path through the legal interpretation and application of this vital part of our religious protections. I'll not go into that history. It can be discovered in a number of excellent books. Suffice it to say that over the years the phrase "separation of church and state" has come to stand in place of the real amendment in application and in most people's minds. As already mentioned, it is a phrase Jefferson used, rather unfortunately in retrospect, in a private letter to a group of Baptists. The courts have seized upon it and over the past several decades gradually substituted it for the real amendment.

Few of the legal minds of our day, however, seem troubled at this astounding alteration of meaning. Most likely this is because it generally pleases them for it to be changed in this way, as it very often (not always) serves the antireligious bias of the secular minds of our day. We have previously noted several Supreme Court justices' warning us about reading a "hostility to religion" into the Constitution; there is good cause for such warnings.

The Religious Ghetto

In essence, Jefferson's separation phrase is used like a club against religious people, usually *conservative* religious people. There seems to be no worry by the intellectual leaders of our day when liberal clerics are active politically. A recent article appearing in the June 30, 1987, edition of the Washington *Times* vividly illustrates my point.

> Delegate Walter Fauntroy had some interesting insights to offer on the indictment of Rep. Harold Ford on umpteen counts of mail fraud in connection with some bank loans. Earlier this month in Memphis at a fundraiser for Mr. Ford, those in attendance were told by Mr. Fauntroy that "Harold is God's servant. . . . If you support him, you will be rewarded."
>
> Mr. Fauntroy, who is also a Baptist minister, said that when Ronald Reagan gets to heaven, the Lord will say: "Depart from Me. When I was hungry you cut food stamps—over Harold Ford's objections—and when I was sick you cut Medicare—over Harold Ford's objections. . . . Depart from Me. In other words, go to hell."
>
> And then Mr. Fauntroy told his audience, "I don't want you to go to hell, so support Harold Ford." In closing, he broke into a song from the musical "The Wiz."

Can you imagine what would have happened had a conservative preacher turned politician made the same comments as did Walter Fauntroy, a liberal preacher turned politician who now represents the District of Columbia in Congress?

Only when conservatives assert their political rights do we suddenly begin to hear dark, ominous warnings about catastrophic violations of the sacred "separation of church and state" dogma. A strange double standard exists in the selective application of the "separation of church and state" hysteria and reproach to religious activity.

Rather than using the First Amendment against

Congress, against whom it was originally and exclusively directed, it is now being used by the secularists of our day as a cattle prod to herd conservative religious people out of the public life of the nation and into, as others have put it, a religious ghetto. Such religious people, it is intimated, are not qualified to participate in the public life of the nation. Or if they must participate, they must dutifully forswear, it seems, letting their religious faith and values play any part in their politics. This could only be accomplished by substituting the separation phrase for the real amendment, and the secularists of our day have been remarkably successful at doing just that.

The Encroaching State, Retreating Church

The net effect of the distortion of the First Amendment is to require that wherever the state is, religion must be excluded. But the state, especially the federal government, has expanded enormously through the decades of our history, far beyond the scope conceived for it by the writers of the Constitution. And if the scope of state involvement is ever expanding and religion must necessarily be excluded wherever it *does* expand, that can only mean that religion's influence must simultaneously be shrinking. Religion is required to give way, to retreat, to withdraw from public life as it has from the public, government-run schools into its churches and synagogues.

However, if some of the secular zealots of our day have their way, religious people will not be exempt from the reach of the state even there. If the state has a compelling interest, and it seems to have an increasing number of them all the time, then it may well just insist that the church do things according to the state's values and standards. There have been court cases where some have sought to coerce churches into hiring people or following policies that are contrary to their long-held beliefs. Why? Because such coercive visionaries believe it right for the state to shape up religious belief according to secular standards.

The chief arena where the expanding control of the state clashes with the historic freedoms of the people, however, is in the public schools. Americans hold widely divergent religious beliefs, and the Constitution guarantees them safety and freedom in those beliefs. Yet we are now told that these beliefs must be removed from the schools, the chief institution for the shaping of young, impressionable minds. These beliefs must be removed because, in contrast to our early years, the schools are now state-run operations.

So, while Judaism and Christianity are forbidden, a value system of subjective, moral neutrality, which is itself a moral and religious position, holds sway and undermines every form of transcendent religion that seeks to inculcate timeless, moral absolutes and values. It's no wonder the schools are so troubled.

Secretary of Education William Bennett has been a forthright spokesman to the nation as a whole and to the educational establishment in particular on the many problems confronting the public schools today. He has not only spoken openly about the mediocre nature of American public education, but he has addressed as well the problems caused when the schools became a battleground over the First Amendment. He has done so, fortunately, with an eye to what the Constitution actually says.

In a speech several years ago, Bennett spoke about the manner in which religious people, in the name of the Constitution, were increasingly being shoved to the back of the social bus. He commented, "The same Constitution that had protected the rights of religious parents, and under whose aegis a host of religions had found happy accommodation, now became, in the hands of aggressive plaintiffs and beguiled judges, the instrument for nothing less than a kind of ghettoizing of religion."[15]

Instead of finding the First Amendment a haven to insure the free exercise of their religious faith in the teaching of values to their children, religious people are now finding that the great amendment is being used to herd them into a social ghetto, separated and walled off from public participation. He went on to observe that the courts "have thrust religion, and things touched by religion out of the public schools; and they have made it far more difficult to give aid to parents of children in private, church-related schools."[16]

Like many other respected public officials, Secretary Bennett is not reluctant to suggest that the Supreme Court has gone astray of the Constitution in its decisions on this matter. He says, "I respectfully submit that the Court has failed to reflect sufficiently on the relationship between our faith and our political order. . . . Our values as a free people and the central values of the Judeo-Christian tradition are flesh of the flesh, blood of the blood."[17]

Bennett, unlike so many today, does not try to pretend that the Founders had no religious belief, nor does he suggest that they divorced their religious beliefs from their statecraft as some seem to think the First Amendment requires. Rather, it is his view that "the attitude that regards 'entanglement' with religion as something akin to entanglement with an infectious disease must be confronted broadly and directly."[18]

He is not simply arguing for a renewed protection of religion in the true, First Amendment sense. He is viewing matters as the Secretary of Education, as one who shares a responsibility for the nation's educational welfare. Bennett feels that the "ghettoizing" of religion has not been especially good for the schools or the public welfare, either. He remarked, "The consequences of this attitude [about religion] for our public schools have been damaging. And these consequences follow from a failure to appreciate a subtle truth about the relationship between religion, the values and habits that religion supports, and the requirements of education among a people charged with self-government."[19] In other words, a nation that wishes to be self-governed desperately needs the values and habits religion promotes in order to accomplish its goal.

This last observation recalls the famous words of the founder of Pennsylvania, William Penn, when he said, "If we will not be governed by God, we must be governed by tyrants."[20] While most decisively rejecting the establishment of a national church, the Founders were equally decisive in their explicit acknowledgment of the fact that our liberties were rooted in the Creator, in nature's God. While they didn't try to say how He should be worshiped, they most assuredly recognized His existence and the relevance of His natural laws to the affairs of mankind.

THE REAL PROBLEM
CAN'T BE SOLVED
PIECEMEAL

As we grope with these numerous First Amendment problems, it becomes increasingly obvious that the current public educational system is the real problem, not the First Amendment. Whether the issue is school prayer, textbook content, or creationism versus evolution, each is without satisfactory solution in the context of a public school system that requires the teaching of values offensive to none, compatible to all.

The hopelessness of these First Amendment problems became especially clear to me during my first campaign for Congress in 1984. In virtually every campaign forum, I was asked my views on school prayer. Each time I responded by stating that I opposed any type of legislation that would dictate the time, the manner, the method, or the words of a prayer. Any such prayer would inevitably offend someone.

As a Christian I also had significant problems with a prayer written by a legislative body so that it could be routinely recited each day in a public school setting. My problem was the result of my understanding of Christ's teachings in His Sermon on the Mount. In that sermon, Christ admonished His followers:

> And when thou prayest, thou shalt not be as the hypocrites are: for they love to pray standing in the synagogues and in the corners of the streets, that they may be seen of men. Verily I say unto you, They have their reward. But thou, when thou prayest, enter into thy closet, and when thou hast shut thy door, pray to thy Father which is in secret; and thy Father which seeth in secret shall reward thee openly. But when ye pray, use not vain repetitions, as the heathen do: for they think that they shall be heard for their much speaking. (Matthew 6:5-7)

Any prayer recited repetitiously and for show is meaningless. Certainly any prayer written by a legislative body and routinely recited by our children who attend public schools would be meaningless. This is especially true since the Supreme Court says it must be exclusively secular in purpose.

I would continue my answer by stating that I do, however, believe children should have the First Amendment right to pray freely, alone or with others, so long as they are not disruptive or violating any rules that apply to any other voluntary or "free time" activities. As a former leader in Young Life, a Christian high school outreach ministry located in many public and private school systems in the United States and abroad, I had experienced firsthand the problems created when public school teachers and administrators are uncertain about what First Amendment activities are now permitted in or around a public school building before, during, or after regular school hours.

Surely children ought to be allowed to gather in a classroom for prayer and Bible study before or after school. Is such an activity, even after the passage of "equal access" legislation, constitutional given the lack of predictability in recent Supreme Court decisions? No one really knows the answer to that question. As a Young Life leader, I was frequently told by public school teachers and administrators that they are afraid of any type of religious activities on their campuses because of their fear that someone would file suit should such activities be permitted. Their fears, of course, are well grounded.

My answer to the school prayer question always concluded with a statement that I support a constitutional amendment that would state that "nothing in the Constitution shall prohibit voluntary school prayer in any public school or public facility nor require participation therein." Simple as such an amendment sounds, what does it mean and how would it apply?

Given the ambiguous guidelines of past Supreme Court cases and the numerous questions regarding practical application that would remain even after such an amendment were ratified, it is apparent that there are no easy or clear-cut legislative or constitutional solutions to the school prayer or other First Amendment issues. So long as we have a public school system that fails to allow free choice by parents and teachers regarding the values and religious beliefs that are taught, the battle will continue and the battlefield will be the classrooms of our public schools.

Again, the real answer rests in establishing a school system, financed with public funds, that will permit such choice. We have done just that with much success in our higher educational system, and eventually, if we are to maintain our First Amendment freedoms and religious pluralism, we must do so in our primary and secondary system as well.

CONCLUSION

As with most of the issues we've discussed, I think we would be well served in this matter if we were to recapture the original meaning and spirit of the Founders when they wrote the First Amendment. It is safe to say that they did not have the restrictive view of religious practice so many today impute to their amendment. The same Congress that passed the First Amendment also set up the congressional chaplaincy system, wherein ministers were to be paid out of the government treasury to say prayers on public property, on public time, at public expense. That practice goes on today in both houses of Congress and the Supreme Court.

We have good reason to be troubled by the state of our religious freedoms today. We've gone a long way down the road from the original amendment; those who have no sympathy for religion are using it to inhibit the free exercise of religion in a variety of ways.

Rather than allowing freedom of religion, we are at best *tolerating* individuals' religious beliefs and practices. Isn't that what people are really suggesting when they say our children don't need to pray in the public schools when they can pray all they want to at home and church? There is, of course, a significant difference between religious freedom and religious tolerance. Justice William O. Douglas warned that we must not try to read into the Bill of Rights "a philosophy of hostility toward religion." That he felt the need to warn against such a prospect tells you where things have been heading in the past few decades.

An informed and aroused citizenry, and one that understands the Founders' intent and our decline from it, is surely the best safeguard of our historic rights. And as Secretary Bennett has said, the view that regards religion as some sort of infectious disease on the body politic "must be confronted broadly and directly." It is my hope that the thoughts set forth in this chapter will have informed and aroused some of my fellow citizens, and that we who care deeply about our historic freedoms and religious beliefs will be up to the confrontation to which we are called in the face of an aggressive secularism that permeates our society.

7

Symptom: A Growing Welfare Dependency

As I sat in my home in Atlanta late one night, I received a phone call from a lady whose voice indicated she was extremely distressed. A better description might be that she was frantic. As I talked to her, I learned that she had been notified by her employer that, in spite of her meager earnings, her wages had been garnisheed by the IRS because of past unpaid federal tax bills.

She was understandably concerned because she had three dependent children and no idea where their father was. Although she had a child-support order from the court that granted her divorce and custody of the children, she had been unable to enforce it. Additionally, she had been plagued by multiple medical bills for herself and her children.

Her point in calling me was to tell me that as a result of the IRS garnishment, she had decided it was in her best interest to simply quit working. She had reached her conclusion after friends had told her that by quitting her job she could actually receive more through accumulated welfare benefits than if she continued working, where she earned just under $14,000 a year.

As I talked further to her, I tried to encourage her to continue working, if for no other reasons than her own pride and the model she needed to provide for her children.

The next day, I went back to the office and checked out her assertion that by quitting work, she could actually receive more benefits through various federal, state, and local welfare programs than she could if she continued to work. To my surprise, I found that her assertion was absolutely correct. I discovered that an individual who earns absolutely zero and has three dependent children would automatically be entitled in 1986 to an annual cash payment of $5,223 from the Aid for Families with Dependent Children program. In addition, she would be entitled to $2,296 in food stamps. On top of those benefits, she would be entitled to Medicaid benefits totalling $2,252, $914 for herself and $446 per child. Additionally, she would qualify for $210 per month in public housing subsidies for a total per year of $2,515, and school lunch subsidies in the amount of $625 for the three children. By receiving all the welfare benefits to which she would be entitled if she had no income, her total standard of living would be $12,911 per year.

How does that compare to the status of an individual who chooses to work every day and earns slightly less than $14,000 per year? In addition to annual food stamp benefits totalling $484, the working mother would be entitled to the same $625 in school lunch subsidies for her three children as the mother who doesn't work. But that's where the similarities end. She would receive no benefits under the Aid to Families with Dependent Children program or from the Medicaid program. And because she worked for a living, she would be required to pay federal taxes of $1,894 and Georgia state taxes of $308. Her total net disposable income, then, would be $12,863. That does not take into account her cost of traveling to and from work, nor does it take into account the cost of day care or any of the other expenses associated with earning a living.

Astonished by what I had found, I was disap-

FIGURE 7.1
POVERTY, UNEMPLOYMENT, AND FEDERAL PUBLIC AID

Year	Poverty Rate	% Change in GNP	Unemployment Rate	Real per Capita Federal Public Aid†
1950	30.2*	8.5	5.3	—
1951	28.0*	10.3	3.3	—
1952	27.9*	3.9	3.0	—
1953	26.2*	4.0	2.9	$ 26.31
1954	27.9*	−1.3	5.5	$ 26.83
1955	24.5*	5.6	4.4	$ 27.98
1956	22.9*	2.1	4.1	$ 28.00
1957	22.8*	1.7	4.3	$ 28.84
1958	23.1*	−0.8	6.8	$ 29.98
1959	22.4	5.8	5.5	$ 33.16
1960	22.2	2.2	5.5	$ 32.64
1961	21.9	2.6	6.7	$ 35.10
1962	21.0	5.3	5.5	$ 40.11
1963	19.5	4.1	5.7	$ 42.75
1964	19.0	5.3	5.2	$ 44.49
1965	17.3	5.8	4.5	$ 48.40
1966	14.7	5.8	3.8	$ 56.57
1967	14.2	2.9	3.8	$ 65.40
1968	12.8	4.1	3.6	$ 76.54
1969	12.1	2.4	3.5	$ 87.22
1970	12.6	−0.3	4.9	$100.19
1971	12.5	2.8	5.9	$127.49
1972	11.9	5.0	5.6	$153.18
1973	11.1	5.2	4.9	$158.25
1974	11.2	−0.5	5.6	$159.62
1975	12.3	−1.3	8.5	$193.10
1976	11.8	4.9	7.7	$216.12
1977	11.6	4.7	7.1	$218.57
1978	11.4	5.3	6.1	$227.19
1979	11.7	2.5	5.8	$222.46
1980	13.0	−0.2	7.1	$216.78
1981	14.0	1.9	7.6	$220.36
1982	15.0	−2.5	9.7	$192.66
1983	15.2	3.6	9.6	$197.54
1984	14.2	6.4	7.5	—
1985	14.0	2.7	7.2	—
1986	13.6	2.5	7.0	—

SOURCE FOR POVERTY RATES: *Money Income and Poverty Status of Families and Persons in the United States: 1985.* Current Population Reports. U.S. Department of Commerce. Bureau of the Census. Table 16. GNP/UNEMPLOYMENT RATES: *Economic Report of the President: 1987.* U.S. Government Printing Office. Washington, D.C., 1987. Tables B-2; B-35. REAL PER CAPITA FEDERAL PUBLIC AID FIGURES: *Poverty, Income Distribution, the Family and Public Policy.* Joint Economic Committee, Congress of the United States. December 19, 1986. Table 5-2.

*For 1950–58, retrospective estimates of the percentage of the population beneath the official poverty level were reported in "Economic Report to the President: Combating Poverty in a Prosperous Economy" (January 1969), reprinted Molly Orshansky, ed., *The* pointed, to say the least, that the lady's conclusion was not only correct, but completely reasonable. Is it any wonder that as the welfare programs and dollars spent to eliminate poverty have increased, so, too, have the number and percentage of Americans dependent on welfare?

THE WAR ON POVERTY—WE LOST

To really understand why this phenomenon has occurred, it's necessary to examine our recent history. Such an examination reveals that the real onset of the increase in poverty can be traced, ironically, to President Lyndon B. Johnson and the advent of his Great Society. I say "ironically" because the Great Society programs were presented to the American people with the promise that they would, if enacted, totally eliminate poverty. The programs were enacted, but poverty has been far from eliminated. In fact, a statistical analysis of what has happened reveals that the only victims of the war on poverty were the very people we supposedly wanted to help.

As can be seen in Figure 7.1, in 1969, the first year most concede that the various antipoverty programs were fully in place and fully funded, 12.1 percent of the American population were living in poverty as the government defined it. Prior to 1969, the Great Society programs had not really had sufficient time to affect poverty one way or the other. By 1981, however, the last year of the Carter Administration's policies, the poverty rate had risen to 14 percent.

Thus, during the twelve-year period when the antipoverty programs of the Great Society were fully

Measure of Poverty, Technical Paper I, vol. 1 (Washington, D.C.: Government Printing Office, n.d.), p. 349.

†The annual figures are measured in constant (1980) dollars. Federal public aid includes Aid for Families with Dependent Children (AFDC), Supplemental Security Income (SSI), Medicaid, food stamps, and certain work training programs.

funded and fully in place, poverty gradually *in-creased*. Conversely, the real smoking gun regarding the failure of the Great Society's antipoverty programs is the fact that during the eighteen-year period preceding the war on poverty, the poverty rate had gradually *declined* from more than 30 percent in 1950 to 12.1 percent in 1969. During the period that the federal government had provided only a safety net for welfare recipients, the poverty rate had been cut in half.

In other words, during the period of time in which we were engaged in this war on poverty, poverty *won;* poverty actually increased in terms of the total percentage of our population, especially among our nation's youth. A number of studies also support this conclusion. One such study was conducted by Ohio University Professors Lowell Gallaway and Richard Vetter. In a recent article, they summarized their findings:

> The rhetoric of the War on Poverty is with us again. The facts are simple: In 1959 the poverty rate for those under age 18 was 26.9%. By 1969 it was 13.8%, an all-time low. In 1984 it stood at 21.1%.
>
> The obvious question is, "What happened on the way to eliminating poverty among the young in our nation?" The answer is straightforward. As currently structured, the welfare system offers the parents of many children a package of benefits, both cash and non-cash, parallel to what they could have by holding a full-time job, but without the work!
>
> What this means is that adults sometimes reject jobs with non-poverty levels of income, in favor of a combination of hard money and non-cash welfare benefits that results in their being regarded by the government as part of the poverty population. This phenomenon has been confirmed in a series of studies in which we have

examined, in an econometric fashion, the relationship between various measures of the poverty rate and the public expenditures designed to reduce that poverty. After taking account of those possible influences on poverty, including the rates of unemployment and economic growth, we find:

1. When federal public assistance to the poor was modest, increases in that assistance reduced poverty, as intended; the aid brought more families above the poverty line.

2. As federal public assistance grew greater, however, the distinctive benefits that aid poses for work-effort became so substantial that the poverty-reducing effects of public aid were overwhelmed by the poverty-increasing, disincentive effects. Boosts in aid caused more, not less, poverty. To an increasing extent the federal government found itself "paying people to be poor." Higher welfare expenditures started to add to the poverty rate after about 1972.

3. The increase in public assistance beyond 1972 levels had added an estimated 5.7 million Americans to the poverty rolls, as more of us, voluntarily, have chosen to be poor.

4. The patterns of individual behavior that have created this situation are not race specific. Whites have been enticed into poverty by higher public-assistance payments as much as blacks, possibly even more so.

Their point is further illustrated by the fact that from 1973 to 1981, the cost in 1980 dollars for public aid per capita shot up 40 percent, from $158 to $220. But the number of persons living in poverty rose from 23 to 32 million, *the first such rise in post-World War II history.*

By contrast, during the 1963 to 1968 period, the number of persons living under the officially established poverty level fell 11 million, even though federal aid per capita in 1980 dollars averaged less than $56, or only 25 percent of the constant-dollar aid level of 1981, and 60 percent below the poverty threshold level. The Galloway and Vetter study shows that federal public aid has created more structual poverty than it has reduced, and that every additional $4,000 of welfare aid has actually added one person to the poverty rolls. In short, the higher the welfare aid levels rose, the more counterproductive they were. Their study also concluded that when social spending began to soar in the 1970s, our nation's economic growth slowed dramatically, and real structural poverty began to rise.

One could argue that if one really looks at this data, all one can conclude for sure is that poverty increased during the war on poverty. Some would even argue that poverty might have increased at even higher rates had it not been for the Great Society programs. The fallacy with that argument, however, is that if you examine the statistics for the period from 1950 to 1969, you will find that poverty as a *percentage* of the total population dropped from 30 percent to 12.1. And after the Reagan Administration slowed the rate of growth in welfare spending, the poverty rate dropped more dramatically than at any time since the war on poverty began.

In other words, when the federal government provided only a safety net, poverty declined. When the federal government began to dramatically increase the number and costs of welfare programs, poverty increased. Such a conclusion is inescapable.

Poverty fell the fastest in the 1960s, when federal social spending averaged only 6 percent of gross national product. It has risen at its most rapid rate since 1978, when social spending reached a peak of 11 percent of gross national product.

Significantly, the sharpest decline in the poverty statistics in the last two decades occurred in 1984, when poverty dropped more than it has in any year since

1968. Not coincidentally, in 1984, two other key economic indicators changed dramatically as well. The gross national product (GNP) increased by 6.4 percent, and the unemployment rate dropped 2.5 percent.

In fact, Figure 7.1 demonstrates that there's a direct correlation between the rate of poverty and the growth in GNP (and the number of jobs created as a result). When our national economy grows, poverty and unemployment decline. When the economy declines, poverty and unemployment increase.

The best antipoverty program we can devise, then, is not another federal welfare program, but rather a strong and vibrant national economy. As can be seen in Figure 7.1, the only sure cure for poverty is economic growth.

BACK TO THE CONSTITUTION

Given these statistics and conclusions, one fundamental question must be asked. Can we continue to justify our failed policies simply because we are well-intentioned? Logic would dictate that given the catastrophic results of those policies, we really have no responsible choice except to reexamine and change them. The question we ought to be debating today is not whether to change our welfare policy, but rather with what do we replace it?

Once again, a good starting point in making such changes is our Constitution. It wisely would keep the federal government away from assuming the responsibility for providing the types of social programs we now have, programs Congress had no constitutional authority to enact, and programs that are now literally contributing to the demise of the American family.

The reason the Constitution placed severe limitations on the powers and scope of the federal government is that the Founding Fathers recognized the importance of the institutions of family, church and synagogue, private associations, businesses, and local and state governments. They also understood that these institutions are more effective in addressing poverty than is the federal government. Aside from their relatively greater efficiency, these institutions are more capable of addressing the spiritual and emotional needs of the poor.

The Founders understood further that the key to economic prosperity and freedom in the United States was for the federal government to protect equal rights and opportunities, not to redistribute earnings and wealth in an attempt to achieve financial equality.

In volume I of William V. Wells's *The Life and Public Service of Samuel Adams,* Wells attributed the following statement to Adams:

> The utopian schemes of leveling [redistribution of the wealth] and a community of goods [central ownership of all the means of production and distribution] are as visionary and impractical as those which vest all property in the Crown. [These ideas] are arbitrary, despotic, and, in our government, unconstitutional.

In a letter to Richard Jackson dated May 5, 1753, Benjamin Franklin expressed a similar attitude about how imprudent welfare policies can encourage dependence. Franklin's attitude was typical of the attitude of most of our Founders.

> Dear Sir:
> I thank you for the kind judicious remarks you have made on my little piece. I have often observed with wonder that temper of the poorer English labourers which you mention, and acknowledge it to be pretty general. When any of them happen to come here, where labour is

much better paid than in England, their industry seems to diminish in equal proportion. But it is not so with the German labourers; they retain the habitual industry and frugality they bring with them, and, receiving higher wages, an accumulation arises that makes them all rich. When I consider, that the English are the offspring of Germans, that the climate they live in is much of the same temperature, and when I see nothing in nature that should create this difference, I am tempted to suspect it must arise from constitution; and I have sometimes doubted whether the laws peculiar to England, which compel the rich to maintain the poor, have not given the latter a dependence, that very much lessens the care of providing against the wants of old age.

I have heard it remarked that the poor in Protestant countries, on the continent of Europe, are generally more industrious than those of Popish countries. May not the more numerous foundations in the latter for relief of the poor have some effect towards rendering them less provident? To relieve the misfortunes of our fellow creatures is concurring with the Deity; it is godlike; but, if we provide encouragement for laziness, and supports for folly, may we not be found fighting against the order of God and Nature, which perhaps has appointed want and misery as all the proper punishments for, and cautions against, as well as necessary consequences of, idleness and extravagance? Whenever we attempt to amend the scheme of Providence, and to interfere with the government of the world, we had need be very circumspect, lest we do more harm than good.

Another problem that Adams, Franklin, and the other Founders feared became particularly clear to me during the 100th Congress. In hearings before the

Housing Subcommittee of the Banking, Finance, and Urban Affairs Committee, on which I serve, testimony was given regarding the latest effort by Congress to address one area of poverty, the homeless. In the various testimonies presented, one in particular stood out to me.

The arresting testimony came from Lt. Col. Ernest A. Miller, Director of National Public Affairs of the Salvation Army, who made a statement regarding separation of church and state. Specifically, he anticipated that some in Congress might be afraid that part of the money appropriated in its homeless bill would ultimately be distributed to churches and religious organizations such as the Salvation Army, and from there it might be used in such a manner as to advance some type of religious belief. His statement in this regard was: "No self-respecting and responsible church group would wish to advance its religious objectives with government funds, most especially at the expense of the poor and homeless."[1]

The tragedy of that testimony is that as the federal government assumes more and more of the responsibility for caring for the needy, it begins necessarily to squeeze out the rightful place of families, individuals, churches, synagogues, and private associations, not only in their responsibility of meeting the physical needs of those who are impoverished, but also in meeting their spiritual needs.

Certainly it's futile to address the physical dimension of poverty without simultaneously dealing with the emotional, psychological, and spiritual dimensions as well. Yet that is precisely what our federal programs are attempting to do. Is it any wonder our past attempts have met with such dismal results?

SUBSIDIZE IT, GET MORE OF IT

The complexity of dealing with an issue such as poverty is undoubtedly part of the reason the Founders restricted the scope of responsibility to be assumed by the federal government. Even without the benefit of statistics regarding the correlation between the increase in federal spending on social programs and the increase in poverty, we ought to understand that when we subsidize something, we will most likely encourage rather than discourage its growth. This is a rule of life: what you subsidize you get more of, and poverty is obviously no exception. Congress certainly understands this concept when it enacts any tax legislation. In passing such bills, there is usually a great deal of discussion about which industries, if any, and what activities, if any, the federal government ought to encourage through subsidies. And how does it provide these subsidies?

The method is various tax credits and tax deductions. One example is the variety of tax incentives given by Congress to the housing industry. By offering tax breaks to individuals and businesses that build low-income housing, Congress has succeeded in increasing the amount of privately funded low-income housing units.

If subsidies have had that effect on low-income housing, why are we surprised by the fact that as we have subsidized poverty, it, too, has increased, our good intentions to the contrary notwithstanding? Why are we surprised that by paying various benefits to mothers with dependent children, the net result has been to increase the number of dependent children? Isn't it equally logical that the number of households headed by a single mother has increased during the same period that our national welfare policy requires a mother to be unmarried or the father to be absent from the home in order for their children to receive benefits?

For the same reason, why are we surprised that we're seeing an incredible increase in the number of teenagers having children out of wedlock at the same time our policies are making illegitimate children a source of additional income? The point is that just as we subsidize certain activities by giving tax credits and tax incentives, so we also subsidize other activities by offering cash payments and benefits to those who are without a job, and even more cash and greater benefits to those who are without jobs *and* have dependent children. In effect, these policies have unwittingly contributed to the demise of the basic family unit. No amount of good intention will ever change these practical results.

In spite of the overwhelming evidence that our current welfare system encourages poverty and dependence, Congress is showing no indication whatsoever that it is aware of the evidence. In fact, Congress appears to be moving in exactly the wrong direction. Rather than changing current welfare programs to encourage able-bodied welfare recipients to obtain a job, it keeps passing new laws to encourage dependence and unemployment.

For example, in June 1987, the Ways and Means Committee in the House passed a bill that it says will encourage able-bodied welfare recipients to get a job as a condition to receiving future benefits. Yet a careful reading of the bill's fine print shows that such able-bodied welfare recipients will be required to take a job only if the job pays more than the combined welfare benefits the recipient is already receiving. Such an approach, while giving lip service to the problem, will, as usual, worsen rather than improve it.

The only way to change the current mess is to understand the value of and need for instilling a work ethic. Wouldn't a better reform measure be to require welfare recipients to take *any* available job no matter what the pay and then, *if* the pay is less than current welfare benefits, the recipients would receive the difference between the amount earned and the total amount of the benefits he or she would have otherwise received? Equally as important, any reform bill must provide that any able-bodied welfare recipient who refuses such work will be refused *any* welfare benefits whatsoever. Such a reform measure wouldn't be nearly as popular, but in the long run it would be infinitely more effective in achieving the real objective. To be effective, charity must be balanced with responsibility.

Going back to my particular constituent's problem, she understood, in spite of the fact that she did not want to become a part of the welfare system, that in the final analysis it made a great deal of sense for her to quit working. Her dilemma is really very typical of the dilemmas many individuals now face.

WHAT'S THE SOLUTION?

It is one thing to point out the problem, but it's another thing entirely to point out the solution. As I have already suggested, the Constitution properly frames the issue in terms of who ought to assume responsibility for addressing the needs of the less fortunate. How do we go about shifting the responsibility for reducing poverty to these other entities, including the welfare beneficiaries themselves?

The answer may well lie in examining President Johnson's vision for eliminating poverty. Although history has proven his vision for America to have been ill-fated, it is nonetheless useful to analyze it in order to find a better vision. Bill Moyers, President Johnson's former press secretary, recently suggested that Johnson himself never intended for his Great Society programs to be unchangeable. In a recent article entitled "A Vested Interest in Poverty," Stuart Butler, director of domestic policy studies at the Heritage Foundation in Washington, D.C., made the following observation:

Lyndon Johnson's Great Society program is 20 years old. Many of its architects gathered in mid-April at the Lyndon Johnson Library in Austin to re-examine LBJ's legacy: Medicaid, Medicare, civil rights legislation, and numerous other landmark programs.

But during that nostalgic reunion, a remark by former Johnson press secretary Bill Moyers inadvertently pointed to what seems to be a structural flaw in the entire Great Society edifice. Lyndon Johnson, recalled Moyers in film footage from an upcoming PBS special previewed at the meeting, once said that his programs should not be considered unchangeable. They should be thought of as writing on a blackboard, the president said.

Unfortunately LBJ's prediction was wrong. The fact is instead of being written in chalk, the programs of the Great Society appear to have been carved in stone. Removing anything from the blackboard has prove[d] virtually impossible, no matter how wasteful or ineffective a program has become. Meanwhile, more and more programs have been added.

The only way to live up to LBJ's vision of the Great Society as a changing set of programs rather than a rigid structure to which things may be added but never taken away, is for liberals to join with conservatives in seeking ways to foster improvement and evolution. For instance, they should support experiments with housing, education and medical vouchers. These would put real financial power into the hands of the beneficiaries, and take it away from the service providers, spurring competition and innovation in human service programs. Just like monopolists in the private sector, the human service monopolists who are funded by the Great Society programs have always opposed vouchers, recognizing them as a threat.

The best way to change the legacy of the failed programs of the Great Society is to offer a new vision (an *old* one, really) consistent with the philosophy incorporated in our Constitution. Specifically, our new vision must recognize that the Great Society programs failed because they unconstitutionally placed the responsibility of meeting human needs on the federal government rather than placing the responsibility where the Constitution placed them.

A recent Los Angeles *Times* survey indicated that the American people understand the need for a new vision for addressing poverty in America. It is not surprising that the survey found Americans to have an enormous sympathy for the poor and their plight on the one hand, and on the other hand no confidence in the federal government's ability to effectively address the problem. What's surprising is that the poor share that view. Nearly 60 percent of all the individuals polled agreed that welfare benefits encourage people to stay poor, and 43 percent of the poor people polled felt the same way, compared with only 31 percent who disagreed. By a 2 to 1 margin the poor agreed, along with the rest, that welfare often encourages husbands to avoid family responsibilities. By a nearly 3 to 1 margin, the poor agreed that young women often have babies so they can collect more welfare.

A REAL-LIFE
SUCCESS STORY

Let me offer one possible new vision for addressing poverty in America. Several years ago, an individual who lived on the outskirts of Atlanta decided to move into one of the areas that is among the most impoverished in the city. He moved there because he had a genuine desire in his heart to minister to the needs of the poor.

After moving, it occurred to him that one of the starting points in his ministry ought to be the distribution of toys, food, and clothing to the needy in his new neighborhood during the Christmas season. With this in mind, he put together a "Toys-for-Tots" type campaign. The concept behind his campaign was that he would go to the churches and synagogues in the more well-to-do suburbs and ask them if they would make contributions of food, clothing, and toys.

After he gathered all the donations together, he invited all the parents and children in the neighborhood to a Christmas party. At the party, when it came time to exchange gifts, each of the children was presented gifts consisting of the food, clothing, and toys that had been donated.

Just as he was about to explode with the joy he felt from seeing the fruits of his labors, he noticed something that a less-sensitive person probably would have never noticed. In a corner of the room were a number of parents who, while certainly happy that their children were able to be the beneficiaries of such a magnanimous gesture, were at the same time torn between conflicting emotions. They were glad to see their children with gifts for Christmas, but they were hurt to know they had been incapable of giving the gifts themselves.

In essence, what my friend saw was that these dads and moms were being stripped of their dignity before his very eyes, and that he had contributed to that result. While no one could criticize his intentions, he was sensitive enough to see the negative as well as the positive results of his small program. After the party had ended, he began to ask himself how he could achieve the same positive results without the negative ones.

Then it occurred to him. He noticed that in this same area were a number of individuals who, though unemployed, were incredibly talented. Some were plumbers. Some were carpenters. Some really had no skill other than the very basic ability of being able to work with their hands. Some could sew. Some could knit. Others could simply clean.

After observing these folks for a while, he conducted a survey in which he asked what each individual could do with the resources he or she had. He also looked around the same neighborhood and found, rather predictably, that there were a lot of needs. Some folks needed plumbing. Some folks needed carpentry work done, and others just needed clothes knitted or someone to help with housekeeping or child care.

After compiling the results of his survey, he began sharing his vision with those who had needs and talents. He explained that while he had little money, he did have an idea about which he thought they could get excited. He explained how, by matching skills with needs, everyone could benefit. As one neighbor who could paint worked on the home of another who couldn't, the one who did the painting would receive a voucher. These vouchers weren't money, but they could be redeemed at the neighborhood store that he created.

Ultimately he went throughout the entire neighborhood until he matched the talent of every person willing and able to work with needs in the community. If a person was able but unwilling to work, that person was not entitled to a voucher or to anything from the community store.

When the next Christmas rolled around, my friend invited the same parents and the same kids and went to the same churches and synagogues and gathered the same types of clothes, food, and toys as had been gathered the year before. He then hosted the same type of party that he had hosted the year before, but with one major difference. This time when it came time to hand out the gifts, it was the parents who were able to give the gifts they had earned through their hard work. At that moment, my friend saw his vision become a reality.

His vision represents a model for America. Just as his creative project worked because it was based on a local assessment of the problem, as well as a local solution, so, too, can similar projects work in other communities.

Elements of Success

My friend's solution worked because it contained three elements essential for success: volunteerism, opportunity, and responsibility. The core of his solicitation and provision of food, clothing, and toys was volunteerism, as was the painting, cleaning, carpentry work, and plumbing. The volunteers' contribution of the gifts, clothing, and toys wasn't enough, however. It was the opportunity to work and be productive and the responsibility attached to that work and productivity that made his vision so effective in meeting the less tangible needs of the community.

Frequently the most creative solutions are local ones. That's what federalism is all about. That's what our Founders were talking about in the Constitution. It wasn't just a document of vague ideas. Our Founders understood that ideas have consequences. Their idea was to allow local communities to address their own problems whenever practicable. Chances are that individuals at the local level are better able to do so than is a central government somewhere far away, like Washington, D.C.

Another element essential to the success of my friend's vision was his understanding that emotional and spiritual needs, as well as physical needs, must be considered. Through his vision, all three needs were at least partially met in his own community. That is something the federal government is incapable of ever doing. In fact, the federal government can actually be counterproductive when it comes to meeting spiritual needs.

My friend had a fundamental understanding that individuals *do* want to help themselves. All they need is the opportunity and the attendant responsibility. Individuals are not likely to take advantage of available opportunities, however, when surrounded by a system that is tugging people in exactly the opposite direction.

In so many ways we have regressed in terms of the vision that this nation once offered to the rest of the world, a world that is starved for a vision. We have regressed because we have abandoned our fundamental understanding that charity and responsibility must go hand in hand.

RESPONSIBLE CHARITY

My first real experience in understanding the relationship between charity and responsibility for the results of my charity, as well as the need for the recipient of my charity to assume certain responsibility, occurred when I was working at my father's used furniture store in downtown Atlanta.

As is still the case in most large cities today, when I was growing up in Atlanta more than twenty years ago, there were always a number of indigent men who approached everyone they saw to beg a quarter, supposedly for a cup of coffee. From time to time one of these men, whom I and my co-workers called "winos," would corner me on the street.

On those occasions when I was cornered, I inevitably gave in and gave the wino a quarter. With the wino on his way, I continued with whatever I was doing, seldom giving the situation another thought until I was again cornered. Sometimes, to avoid confrontation, I would vary my path by as much as a block.

One day when I was cornered directly in front of my father's store, I gave in, as usual, to the wino's request. Unbeknownst to me, my father had been watching my act of charity from inside the store. When I came inside, he asked me why I had given the wino a quarter of my hard-earned money when all he would do is go and buy another bottle of wine and, thanks to me, be worse off than before.

I reacted to my father's statement with anger and

disappointment. I was angry that he would chastise me for my charity, and disappointed that he had become so callous as to suggest the wino wouldn't use the quarter to buy coffee. As I reflected on the feeling of self-satisfaction I had experienced as a result of my charity, I was particularly resentful of my father's suggestion that the wino was worse off because of my gift than he would have been had I kept my money.

Determined to prove my father wrong, I decided that the next time I gave a quarter to a wino, I would follow him to see how he spent it. My chance came several days later. After giving a wino a quarter, I followed him, being careful to make certain he didn't see me. To my great relief, he went straight into the small grocery store located just down the block from my father's store. I was relieved because I knew the store did not sell wine, beer, or liquor.

As I stood outside peering into the window, however, I was surprised to see him purchase a bottle of cheap after shave lotion. I was surprised because I had never noticed any wino smelling particularly pleasant!

After completing his purchase, the wino walked down the street, turned the corner, and proceeded into the alley directly behind our store. Still making certain that the wino was unaware I was following him, I stood at the end of the alley and watched as he removed the bottle of after shave from his back pocket.

As he opened it, I remembered all the times my brother and I had shoveled countless numbers of empty after shave bottles into trash cans as we cleaned the alley. I had always wondered why there was such an abundance of them. Seeing him open the bottle and drink its contents, I understood for the first time why there were so many empty bottles and why my father had said what he did.

As a result of that incident, I had a better understanding about the necessity of combining responsibility and accountability with charity, no matter how well-intended the act of charity might be.

Both the responsibility for how my money was spent and the results of the expenditure had been missing in my act of charity. What was also missing was "tough love," which is a type of love that's accompanied by a willingness to take the time to understand the underlying problem causing poverty or alcoholism or drug abuse. It means being tough enough with the person you're trying to help to hold him accountable for his actions, even as you try to help him overcome the real problem. Today too many are unwilling to recognize that a significant part of the responsibility for poverty rests on the person in poverty.

In my frequent encounters with winos, I had been sensitive enough to care about their problem, but not sensitive enough or caring enough to take the time to determine the root cause or hold the wino accountable for his own actions.

In so many ways, our federal welfare programs have lacked in exactly the same ways. Part of the reason, as we've already discussed, is that the federal government is ill-equipped to address the real problems responsibly. Another part of the problem has been a failure of leadership in the private sector, especially among families, churches, and businesses.

If we're to turn this around, we must offer more visions like the one of my friend who reformed a "toys for tots" type campaign into a "dignity for dads" type campaign. With this responsibility in mind, I recently established a private foundation, funded entirely by the private sector, to promote volunteer solutions to the problems the federal government has failed to solve.

FAVOR

The foundation, entitled Foundation for the Advancement of Volunteerism, Opportunity, and Responsibility (FAVOR), is initially focusing on three specific problems: homelessness, legal services for the indigent, and housing and care for unwed, single mothers. The whole concept behind FAVOR is to demonstrate by example that we can meet the legitimate needs that must be met in this country without the intervention of the federal government.

An Alternative to "Throwing Money at the Problems"

Rather than addressing these problems by spending inordinate amounts of money, FAVOR offers creative approaches to the problems it addresses. In contrast to the approach recently taken by Congress when it authorized over $1 billion to address the problem of homelessness, FAVOR encourages the use of existing resources.

Though Congress, as usual, was quick to spend the American taxpayers' money to address the homeless issue, it has no real plan for addressing the spiritual and emotional problems that frequently cause people to be homeless in the first place.

In contrast, FAVOR's approach is to encourage churches and synagogues in my congressional district that don't already have a ministry to the homeless to establish one. Because most churches and synagogues have education wings that are primarily used only on Saturdays, Sundays, and Wednesday evenings, they already have the most costly portion of their homeless ministry. By forming a special homeless ministry comprising thirty-five or more couples who are willing to donate one night a month to open the doors to the otherwise unused building and stay through the night, both shelter and personal counseling can be provided.

Many of the homeless are only temporarily homeless. Some have experienced an unexpected, temporary job loss. Others have moved from their previous hometown to take a new job, but until they receive the first paycheck, they can't afford housing or food.

The majority of the homeless, however, are that way because of mental disorders, drug or alcohol abuse, or a combination of the two. These are the people who need more than physical shelter. FAVOR continues to encourage private solutions to these long-term, underlying problems.

A Private Legal Services Alternative

Legal services for the indigent is another problem Congress has tried to solve with money. Millions of dollars have been spent with little result on programs like the Legal Services Corporation. The majority of the money has been spent on administrative overhead, physical facilities to house the administrators, and lobbying efforts on behalf of liberal causes.

FAVOR's approach to addressing the real problem is a truly voluntary group of attorneys in private practice. Specifically, fifty-two attorneys donate one week each year to FAVOR. During that week, the attorney agrees to accept any cases referred to him. The only cases accepted are those involving indigent clients who could not otherwise afford to retain legal help. And any case referred to the volunteer attorney during that week of service becomes his or her responsibility until the case has been resolved. Under this system, there is an equitable distribution of the workload and a continuity of legal counsel for the clients.

An Alternative for Unwed Mothers

The final focus of FAVOR is on the needs of unwed, single mothers. As I have mentioned previously, there are actually three victims in every abortion—the child, the mother, and the thousands of parents who wait for years to adopt an infant child. To oppose abortion without at the same time offering an alternative is irresponsible.

In order to offer a realistic alternative, FAVOR encourages families to open their homes to unwed mothers during their pregnancies. By affording the unwed mothers a home as well as much-needed emotional support, FAVOR seeks to reduce the number of abortions that result because the unwed mother lacks such help.

A Model for Other Districts

In a nutshell, I believe it is possible for each of our 435 congressional districts to meet the needs that Congress attempts unsuccessfully to solve with money. With this in mind, FAVOR is designed to prove by example that the philosophy upon which our Constitution was based can work again.

The basic principle of division of responsibilities between individual, family, church, and private sector institutions has worked well. But in our zeal, and quite frankly in our ignorance of our own Constitution, we have ignored those principles to the point that we are now seriously jeopardizing the very existence of our constitutional republic.

As a nation, we can no longer afford to allow Congress to operate under the Machiavellian notion that the end justifies any means, even if the means is to totally ignore the limitations placed on the federal government by the Constitution. The real tragedy of this approach is that rather than achieving the intended result, it has achieved exactly the opposite.

MAKING A FEDERAL CASE
OUT OF EVERYTHING

Our nation was founded on the principle that the first places you should turn to for help are your family, your church, and your neighbors. Now, the first place we seem to turn to is the federal government. As we have become increasingly dependent on the federal government and its programs to solve virtually every social problem, a role not assigned to it by the Constitution, we have correspondingly failed to demand that the federal government assume the very responsibility the Constitution *does* place on it. We have been remiss in requiring that it establish and administer justice.

Consider my constituent who had three children and whose husband was legally and morally responsible for his own children's support. Though she had a court order mandating that her ex-husband pay for a portion of their children's support, her repeated attempts to enforce the decree had failed. Consequently, he had escaped his responsibility. In short, she felt powerless to do anything about the problem except quit work and rely on the federal government to assume the responsibility her children's own father refused.

Rather than creating more programs and policies that encourage poverty, the federal government, through the Justice Department, ought to make absolutely certain that when a father in this country has any type of obligation to his children, if he will not assume it out of a sense of moral consciousness or responsibility, he must be *forced* to assume it.

Through the enforcement of laws like the Uniform Reciprocal Child Support Act, a law already on the books in most states, this can be accomplished. But like so many of the programs within the Justice Department, too little money is available for law enforcement because of the exorbitant amount being spent on social programs that increase rather than decrease the real problems.

If we're going to reduce poverty, we're going to have to radically rethink our current policies. I can think of no more radical thought than applying the principles set forth in the Constitution.

By shifting the primary responsibility for meeting the needs of the indigent and disabled to the family, churches, private charities, and local and state governments, the physical and spiritual needs can be more effectively met, and the federal government can get back into the business of administering justice and providing for the general welfare and national defense.

To accomplish this objective, families, churches, and local governments must step forward and accept their rightful responsibilities. There are those who may argue that these other institutions won't step forward, and they are probably correct so long as we maintain our current national budget structure. This is true primarily because our track record has thus far demonstrated that the more the federal government assumes responsibilities not delegated to it, the more other parts of society yield to their preemption. Given the federal government's dismal performance, however, we really can't afford *not* to reduce its role in providing solutions to the welfare dilemma. This is so not only because it currently costs so much in terms of dollars and cents, but also because it currently costs so much in human terms.

Is it compassionate to continue programs that increase rather than decrease the poverty rate? that discourage rather than encourage self-sufficiency? that contribute to the demise rather than the strengthening of the American family? Of course not! In the name of compassion, we must recapture our winning formula, because it offers America the vision so badly needed as she begins her third century as a constitutional republic.

8

The Cure: A Return to the Original Formula

As we have seen, when the federal government assumes only the responsibilities for which it was established, it achieves its best results. At the same time, the other American institutions that comprise our nation—our families, churches, synagogues, private charities, businesses, and local and state governments—then have the resources to assume and address the responsibilities they retained under our Constitution.

Many today who desire to rewrite our Constitution in ways never permitted by the Constitution itself, justify their actions by arguing that at the time the Constitution was written we were a smaller and less diverse nation. They maintain that our size and diversity now necessitate a different national blueprint.

This argument is undoubtedly the same argument that the experts at Coca Cola made when they persuaded the management to change its original philosophy and formula just before that company's 100th anniversary. Coca Cola had grown tremendously since its inception, and during its period of huge growth it had become more diversified as well.

The fallacy with the experts' argument, both in the case of Coca Cola and that of the United States, is that it fails to recognize that the original philosophy and formula had allowed the growth and diversification in the first place. If the original formulas were so flawed, why did Coca Cola and the United States prosper as they did? Argue as they will, history speaks for itself. Our nation's original formula, our Constitution, has served us well. As we have seen, the disastrous results of abandoning our original formula require us to reembrace it.

WE'VE ONLY JUST BEGUN

During the past several years, under the Reagan Administration, we have begun the gradual process of returning to the original formula. In his first inaugural address, President Reagan called on the Congress and the American people to return to "federalism," to get back to the basics.

Though Congress has fought the president and his supporters in Congress every step of the way, we are already seeing the fruits of our change in direction. Just as Coca Cola, after returning to its original formula, saw its sales return to their previous high levels and then soar beyond, America, under President Reagan's policies, has seen public education improve, the rate of poverty decline, productivity increase, a record number of new jobs created and, in short, an encouraging trend toward renewed prosperity and national pride. These are just a handful of the recent successes we have enjoyed, not by embracing our original formula, but by simply moving closer to it. Imagine what would happen if we reembraced it totally.

OBSTACLES REMAIN

Despite our recent successes, much remains to be done. There are still many symptoms being misdiagnosed. Too many in Congress still believe, despite the overwhelming evidence to the contrary, that more federal programs and more federal spending is the solution rather than the problem. They are blind to the fact that the mediocrity typifying our public schools in the past is the result of the system itself, a system built and sustained by the educational experts who have used it to promote their own brand of secularism and in the process abandoned instruction in the basic areas of reading, writing, and computing.

There are those who still believe that the way to end poverty is to subsidize it. They honestly believe that so long as they are well intentioned in their approach the results can be ignored, even if the consequence is to create a new generation of individuals who are as dependent on the federal government and its programs as black slaves were once dependent on their masters.

Today, as we have moved away from the basic constitutional principles with which we started, we have become too dependent upon federal programs for virtually every problem that can be identified. It seems that as soon as any problem is mentioned on television or in the newspaper, an instant legislative solution is offered. Typically, that solution is to create and fund another federal program, and if that program doesn't work, simply create another larger and more expensive one.

TOWARD A UNIFIED HOUSE

Today America is truly a nation divided. She is divided between two world views. One is the view our Founders chose. It is a world view that recognizes the existence of a Creator God from whom our liberties and rights have come, and that there is a need for the state to protect those unalienable rights, and a need for a balance between the responsibilities of the federal government and the responsibilities of the people, those of the states, and those of local governments. The other is a man-centered world view, a world view in which life is accidental and absolutes are nonexistent. Human rights and liberties are the prerogatives of the state, to be given and taken at the government's discretion. It is a view in which virtually every problem must be solved through federal programs, no matter how inefficiently, ineffectively, or costly.

In the final analysis, Lincoln's warning about a house divided remains applicable today. America cannot remain a house divided between these two conflicting and irreconcilable world views. She must embrace one or the other, and she'd best choose carefully. Many consequences, for good or ill, will follow her choice, and the one she embraces will decide the kind of world in which our children and our children's children will live.

Notes

Introduction

1. Max Farrand, ed., *The Records of the Federal Convention* (New Haven: Yale University Press, 1937), vol. 3, p. 450.

Chapter 2

1. Abraham Lincoln, "A House Divided": Speech at Springfield, Illinois, June 16, 1858, in *The Collected Works of Abraham Lincoln,* Roy P. Basler, ed. (New Brunswick, N.J.: Rutgers University Press, 1953), p. 461.

2. Sir William Blackstone, *Commentaries on the Laws of England,* 4 vols., Chitty ed. (New York: W. E. Dean, Printer & Publisher, 1852), vol. 1, p. 26.

3. Ibid., p. 28.

4. William Simon, *A Time for Truth* (New York: Reader's Digest Press, 1978), p. 124.

5. Attributed to James Madison. As quoted in *Progressive Calvinism,* Frederick Nymeyer, ed. (South Holland, Ill.: Progressive Calvinism League, 1958), vol. 1, no. 1, p. 31. John Quincy Adams, while serving as Secretary of State, made a similar statement in an oration celebrating July 4, 1821. He said, "From the day of the Declaration . . . They [the American people] were bound by the laws of God, which they all, and by the laws of the Gospel, which they nearly all, acknowledged as the rules of their conduct." Adams' quotation is in Hamilton Albert Long's *The*

American Ideal of 1776: The Twelve Basic American Principles (Philadelphia: Your Heritage Books, Inc., 1976), p. 4. Adams' speech itself is included, in part, in *John Quincy Adams and American Continental Empire: Letters, Papers, and Speeches,* Walter LaFeber, ed. (Chicago: Quandrangle Books, 1965), pp. 42–46.

Chapter 3

1. *Dred Scott v. John F. A. Sanford,* United States Supreme Court, December Term, 1856, pp. 404–410.

2. Attributed to George Mason, June 12, 1776. As quoted in *Fifth Annual Independence Day Celebration Kit* (Marlborough, N.H.: Plymouth Rock Foundation, n.d.). A few years earlier, the Massachusetts House of Representatives had made the following resolution: "Resolved, that the inhabitants of this Province are unalienably entitled to those essential rights ('founded in the law of God and Nature') in common with all men: in that no law of society can, consistent with the law of God and nature, divest them of those rights." From *Resolutions of House of Representative,* Massachusetts, 1765, as quoted in *The American Ideal of 1776,* p. 22.

3. James D. Richardson, ed., *Messages and Papers of the Presidents* (Washington, D.C.: Bureau of National Literature and Art, 1910), vol. 5, pp. 3210–3211.

Chapter 4

1. George Seldes, ed., *The Great Quotations* (New York: Pocket Books, 1972), p. 444.

2. Ibid., p. 455.

Chapter 5

1. Seldes, *The Great Quotations,* p. 200.

2. Article VI, clause 14, of Mr. Pinckney's proposed plan. Recorded in the *Journal of the Federal*

Convention, kept by James Madison. Edited by E. H. Scott. (Chicago: Albert, Scott & Co., 1893. Reprinted from the edition of 1840, which was published under the direction of the United States Government from the original manuscripts), p. 68.

    3. Richardson, *Messages and Papers,* vol. 1, p. 367.

    4. Ibid., p. 398.

    5. *The Congressional Globe,* 5 June 1866, 2966, as quoted in *The Constitution and Federal Jurisdiction in American Education,* Kerry L. Morgan, Esq. (Virginia Beach, Va.: CBN University, 1985), pp. 27–28.

    6. *The Congressional Globe,* 2968, as quoted in *Federal Jurisdiction,* Morgan, p. 30.

    7. *The Congressional Globe,* 2969, as quoted in *Federal Jurisdiction,* Morgan, p. 30.

    8. Marcella D. Hadeed, "The Politicization of the Classroom" in *A Blueprint for Education Reform,* Connaught Marshner, ed. (Chicago: Regnery Gateway, Free Congress Research and Education Foundation, 1984), pp. 111–113.

Chapter 6

    1. *Zorach v. Clauson,* 343 U.S. 306, 313 (1952).

    2. *Engel v. Vitale,* 370 U.S. 421 (1962).

    3. *Abingdon v. Schempp,* 374 U.S. 203 (1963).

    4. *Lemon v. Kurtzman,* 403 U.S. 602, 612 (1971).

    5. *Wallace v. Jaffree,* 472 U.S. 38 (1985).

    6. Thomas Jefferson, *Bill for Establishing Elementary Schools,* section 10, line 3. As recorded in *Early History of the University of Virginia,* contained in *The Letters of Thomas Jefferson and Joseph C. Cabell,* hitherto unpublished; with an Appendix consisting of Mr. Jefferson's Bill for a Complete System of Education, and other illustrative documents; and an introduction, comprising a brief historical sketch of the university, and a biographical notice of

Joseph C. Cabell. Entered, according to act of Congress, in the year 1856, by J. W. Randolph, in the Clerk's Office of the District Court of the United States for the Eastern District of Virginia (Richmond: C. H. Wynne, 1856), pp. 96–97.

7. *Wallace v. Jaffree, Supra* at 62.

8. *The Northwest Ordinance of 1787,* quoted in its entirety in *Documents of American History,* Henry Steele Commager, Ninth Edition (Englewood Cliffs, N.J.: Prentice-Hall, Inc., 1973), p. 131.

9. Alexis de Tocqueville, *Democracy in America,* eds. J. P. Mayer and Max Lerner, trans. George Lawrence (New York: Harper & Row, Publishers, 1966), p. 278.

10. Robert Moynard Hutchins, ed., *Great Books of the Western World* (Chicago, Ill.: Encyclopedia Britannica Educational Corporation, 1952), vol. 2, p. 561.

11. Fuller and Tippo, *College Botany* (New York: Holt, Rinehart & Winston, 1961), p. 25.

12. The Atlanta *Journal Constitution,* June 6, 1985, p. 9A.

13. *Zorach v. Clauson,* 343 U.S. 306, 313 (1952).

14. Richardson, *Messages and Papers,* vol. 1, p. 44.

15. David Wagner, "Bill Bennett's Dilemma" in *The National Review,* June 19, 1987, p. 30.

16. Ibid.

17. Ibid.

18. Ibid.

19. Ibid.

20. Seldes, *The Great Quotations,* p. 450.

Chapter 7

1. Lt. Colonel Ernest A. Miller, Director, National Public Affairs, the Salvation Army. Testimony before the United States House of Representatives Subcommittee on Housing and Community Development, February 4, 1987.